SUSPENSION
AND STEERING

Tasksheet Manual for
NATEF Proficiency

CDX Automotive

JONES AND BARTLETT PUBLISHERS

Sudbury, Massachusetts

BOSTON   TORONTO   LONDON   SINGAPORE

World Headquarters

Jones and Bartlett Publishers
40 Tall Pine Drive
Sudbury, MA 01776
978-443-5000
info@jbpub.com
www.jbpub.com

Jones and Bartlett Publishers
Canada
6339 Ormindale Way
Mississauga, Ontario L5V 1J2
Canada

Jones and Bartlett Publishers
International
Barb House, Barb Mews
London W6 7PA
United Kingdom

Jones and Bartlett's books and products are available through most bookstores and online booksellers. To contact Jones and Bartlett Publishers directly, call 800-832-0034, fax 978-443-8000, or visit our website, www.jbpub.com.

Substantial discounts on bulk quantities of Jones and Bartlett's publications are available to corporations, professional associations, and other qualified organizations. For details and specific discount information, contact the special sales department at Jones and Bartlett via the above contact information or send an email to specialsales@jbpub.com.

Production Credits

Chief Executive Officer: Clayton Jones
Chief Operating Officer: Don W. Jones, Jr.
President, Higher Education and Professional Publishing: Robert W. Holland, Jr.
Sr. V.P., Sales and Marketing: James Homer
V.P., Design and Production: Anne Spencer
V.P., Manufacturing and Inventory Control: Therese Connell
Publisher: Kimberly Brophy
Acquisitions Editor–Automotive: Martin Schumacher
Associate Editor: Amanda Brandt
Editorial Assistant: Kara Ebrahim
Production Manager: Jenny L. Corriveau
Director of Marketing: Alisha Weisman
Associate Marketing Manager: Jessica Cormier
Cover Design: Scott Moden
Cover Image: © Mashe/Dreamstime.com
Composition: Shepherd, Inc.
Printing and Binding: Courier Kendallville
Cover Printing: Courier Kendallville

The procedures and protocols in this book are based on the most current recommendations of responsible sources. The publisher, however, makes no guarantee as to, and assume no responsibility for, the correctness, sufficiency, or completeness of such information or recommendations. Other or additional safety measures may be required under particular circumstances.

For every task in ASE 4: Suspension and Steering, the following safety requirement must be strictly followed: Comply with personal and environmental safety practices associated with clothing; eye protection; hand tools; power equipment; proper ventilation; and the handling, storage, and disposal of chemicals/materials in accordance with local, state, and federal safety and environmental regulations.

6048
Printed in the United States of America
15 14 13 12   10 9 8 7 6 5 4 3

Contents

Resource Preview

2008 NATEF and CDX tasksheet numbers appear at the beginning and end of every task, as well as in the general information for the section.

Required and recommended materials and equipment are listed for each task.

Safety issues relevant to the tasks are listed at the beginning of every section.

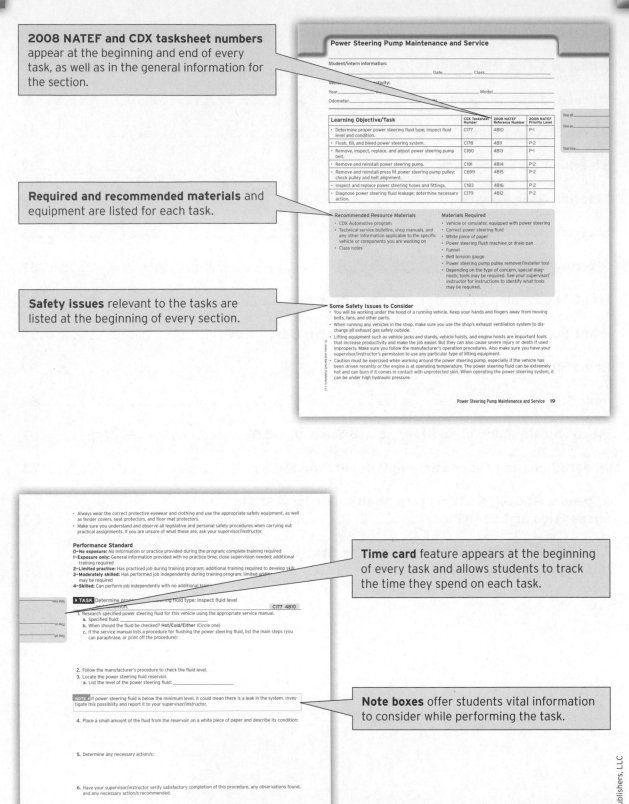

Power Steering Pump Maintenance and Service

Student/intern information:

Date_____ Class_____

Vehicle used for this activity:

Year_____ Make_____ Model_____

Odometer_____ VIN_____

Time off_____

Time on_____

Total time_____

Learning Objective/Task	CDX Tasksheet Number	2008 NATEF Reference Number	2008 NATEF Priority Level
• Determine proper power steering fluid type; inspect fluid level and condition.	C177	4B10	P-1
• Flush, fill, and bleed power steering system.	C178	4B11	P-2
• Remove, inspect, replace, and adjust power steering pump belt.	C180	4B13	P-1
• Remove and reinstall power steering pump.	C181	4B14	P-2
• Remove and reinstall press fit power steering pump pulley; check pulley and belt alignment.	C699	4B15	P-2
• Inspect and replace power steering hoses and fittings.	C183	4B16	P-2
• Diagnose power steering fluid leakage; determine necessary action.	C179	4B12	P-2

Recommended Resource Materials
- CDX Automotive program
- Technical service bulletins, shop manuals, and any other information applicable to the specific vehicle or components you are working on
- Class notes

Materials Required
- Vehicle or simulator, equipped with power steering
- Correct power steering fluid
- White piece of paper
- Power steering flush machine or drain pan
- Funnel
- Belt tension gauge
- Power steering pump pulley remover/installer tool
- Depending on the type of concern, special diagnostic tools may be required. See your supervisor/instructor for instructions to identify what tools may be required.

Some Safety Issues to Consider
- You will be working under the hood of a running vehicle. Keep your hands and fingers away from moving belts, fans, and other parts.
- When running any vehicles in the shop, make sure you use the shop's exhaust ventilation system to discharge all exhaust gas safely outside.
- Lifting equipment such as vehicle jacks and stands, vehicle hoists, and engine hoists are important tools that increase productivity and make the job easier. But they can also cause severe injury or death if used improperly. Make sure you follow the manufacturer's operation procedures. Also make sure you have your supervisor/instructor's permission to use any particular type of lifting equipment.
- Caution must be exercised when working around the power steering pump, especially if the vehicle has been driven recently or the engine is at operating temperature. The power steering fluid can be extremely hot and can burn if it comes in contact with unprotected skin. When operating the power steering system, it can be under high hydraulic pressure.

Power Steering Pump Maintenance and Service   **19**

- Always wear the correct protective eyewear and clothing and use the appropriate safety equipment, as well as fender covers, seat protectors, and floor mat protectors.
- Make sure you understand and observe all legislative and personal safety procedures when carrying out practical assignments. If you are unsure of what these are, ask your supervisor/instructor.

Performance Standard
0–No exposure: No information or practice provided during the program; complete training required
1–Exposure only: General information provided with no practice time; close supervision needed; additional training required
2–Limited practice: Has practiced job during training program; additional training required to develop skill
3–Moderately skilled: Has performed job independently during training program; limited additional training may be required
4–Skilled: Can perform job independently with no additional training

▶ **TASK** Determine proper power steering fluid type; inspect fluid level and condition.   C177 4B10

1. Research specified power steering fluid for this vehicle using the appropriate service manual.
   a. Specified fluid: _____
   b. When should the fluid be checked? **Hot/Cold/Either** (Circle one)
   c. If the service manual lists a procedure for flushing the power steering fluid, list the main steps (you can paraphrase, or print off the procedure):

2. Follow the manufacturer's procedure to check the fluid level.
3. Locate the power steering fluid reservoir.
   a. List the level of the power steering fluid: _____

NOTE If power steering fluid is below the minimum level, it could mean there is a leak in the system. Investigate this possibility and report it to your supervisor/instructor.

4. Place a small amount of the fluid from the reservoir on a white piece of paper and describe its condition:

5. Determine any necessary action/s:

6. Have your supervisor/instructor verify satisfactory completion of this procedure, any observations found, and any necessary action/s recommended.

Performance Rating

CDX Tasksheet Number: C177   2008 NATEF Reference Number: 4B10

☐ 0   ☐ 1   ☐ 2   ☐ 3   ☐ 4

Supervisor/instructor signature _____   Date _____

20   Power Steering Pump Maintenance and Service

Time card feature appears at the beginning of every task and allows students to track the time they spend on each task.

Note boxes offer students vital information to consider while performing the task.

Performance standard and rating areas simplify the sign-off process for instructors.

Acknowledgments

Jones and Bartlett Publishers would like to thank the following contributor and reviewers for their assistance with this manual:

Contributor:
Kirk VanGelder, CMAT & L1, NATEF ETL
AYES Instructor
Clark County Skills Center
Vancouver, Washington

Reviewers:
Edward J. Heim
ASE certified in Automotive and Automotive Machinist
Battle Ground High School
Battle Ground, Washington

Marty Kamimoto
Fresno City College
Fresno, California

Sonny Reeves, CMAT, NATEF ETL
AYES Instructor
Hutchings Career Center
Macon, Georgia

Jim Stafford
Tennessee Technology Center—Newbern
Newbern, Tennessee

CD**X** Automotive

Designed to help automotive programs meet NATEF requirements, this interactive automotive training system introduces students to the fundamental principles and applications of automotive education. It also equips instructors with a complete set of easy-to-use course materials. This innovative resource will enrich your conventional course, or can be used as a primary management source to deliver an online program that accommodates increasing student enrollments.

CDX Automotive improves learning outcomes in automotive education by increasing student engagement and performance through personalized learning. Key features include:
- Course content mapped to the 8 ASE test areas
- Easy and intuitive navigation
- Over 850 automotive procedural and demonstration videos, including content on timely topics such as alternative fuels
- Unlimited practice tests, knowledge check exercises, and final exams that are automatically scored and recorded to save time and eliminate human error
- Support for both 2005 and 2008 NATEF standards with tasksheets and updated tasksheet reporting, making ASE recertification even easier for instructors nationwide
- *CDX Automotive Access Pack* option for students looking to purchase required or recommended access to **CDX Automotive** from their local college bookstore

CDX Automotive includes easy-to-use and state-of-the-art learning performance management tools to help schools manage and report student performance data that meet NATEF's ASE e-learning certification requirements. **CDX Automotive** offers a turnkey solution to high schools, vocational schools, community colleges and skill centers wishing to join the e-learning initiative announced by NATEF that allows programs to qualify for reduced curriculum hour requirements through e-learning completed outside of regular program hours.

Steer your course in the direction you want with **CDX Automotive**.

Request a free trial at www.cdxauto.com.

Vehicle, Customer, and Service Information

Student/intern information:

Name_____ Date_____ Class_____

Vehicle used for this activity:

Year_____ Make_____ Model_____

Odometer_____ VIN _____

Time off_____

Time on_____

Total time_____

Learning Objective/Task	CDX Tasksheet Number	2008 NATEF Reference Number	2008 NATEF Priority Level
• Complete work order to include customer information, vehicle identifying information, customer concern, related service history, cause, and correction.	C879	4A1	P-1
• Locate and interpret vehicle and major component identification numbers.	C872	4A4	P-1
• Research applicable vehicle and service information, such as suspension and steering system operation, vehicle service history, service precautions, and technical service bulletins.	C166	4A3	P-1
• Identify and interpret suspension and steering system concerns; determine necessary action.	C851	4A2	P-1

Recommended Resource Materials

- CDX Automotive program
- Technical service bulletins, shop manuals, and any other information applicable to the specific vehicle or components you are working on
- Class notes

Materials Required

- Blank work order
- Vehicle with available service history records
- Depending on the type of concern, special diagnostic tools may be required. See your supervisor/instructor for instructions to identify what tools may be required.

Some Safety Issues to Consider

- Diagnosis of this fault may require test driving the vehicle on the school grounds. Attempt this task only with full permission from your instructor and follow all the guidelines exactly.
- When running any vehicles in the shop, make sure you use the shop's exhaust ventilation system to discharge all exhaust gas safely outside.
- Lifting equipment such as vehicle jacks and stands, vehicle hoists, and engine hoists are important tools that increase productivity and make the job easier. But they can also cause severe injury or death if used improperly. Make sure you follow the manufacturer's operation procedures. Also, make sure you have your supervisor/instructor's permission to use any particular type of lifting equipment.
- Always wear the correct protective eyewear and clothing and use the appropriate safety equipment, as well as fender covers, seat protectors, and floor mat protectors.
- Make sure you understand and observe all legislative and personal safety procedures when carrying out practical assignments. If you are unsure of what these are, ask your supervisor/instructor.

Performance Standard

0—No exposure: No information or practice provided during the program; complete training required

1—Exposure only: General information provided with no practice time; close supervision needed; additional training required

2—Limited practice: Has practiced job during training program; additional training required to develop skill

3—Moderately skilled: Has performed job independently during training program; limited additional training may be required

4—Skilled: Can perform job independently with no additional training

▶ **TASK** Complete work order to include customer information, vehicle identifying information, customer concern, related service history, cause, and correction. **C879 4A1**

1. Complete the work order specifying:
   a. Customer information
   b. Customer concern
   c. Vehicle identifying information
   d. Any related service history, etc.

The rest of this task is completed by performing the remainder of the tasks, and can be signed off at the end of this tasksheet. Please refer to page 4 for the completion of this task.

▶ **TASK** Locate and interpret vehicle and major component identification numbers. **C872 4A4**

1. Using the VIN for identification, access the appropriate technical information source to identify the following:
   a. VIN: _____

2. Look up the VIN in the appropriate service manual and identify the following information:
   a. Country of origin: _____
   b. Plant: _____
   c. Type of restraint system: _____
   d. Engine: _____
   e. Model year: _____

3. List the location of any certification and calibration decals:

4. Describe the main information on each decal:

5. Have your supervisor/instructor verify satisfactory completion of this procedure, any observations found, and any necessary action/s recommended.

Performance Rating

		CDX Tasksheet Number: C872	2008 NATEF Reference Number: 4A4	
☐	☐	☐	☐	☐
0	1	2	3	4

Supervisor/instructor signature _____ Date_____

▶ **TASK** Research applicable vehicle and service information, such as suspension and steering system operation, vehicle service history, service precautions, and technical service bulletins. **C166 4A3**

1. Using the VIN for identification, use the appropriate source to access the vehicle's service history in relation to prior related suspension and steering system work or customer concerns.
   a. List any related repairs/concerns, and their dates:

2. Using the VIN for identification, access any relevant technical service bulletins for the particular vehicle you are working on in relation to steering and suspension updates or other service issues.
   a. List any related service bulletins:

3. Have your supervisor/instructor verify satisfactory completion of this procedure, any observations found, and any necessary action/s recommended.

Performance Rating

CDX Tasksheet Number: C166   2008 NATEF Reference Number: 4A3

☐ 0   ☐ 1   ☐ 2   ☐ 3   ☐ 4

Supervisor/instructor signature _____ Date_____

▶ **TASK** Identify and interpret suspension and steering system concerns; determine necessary action.

C851 4A2

Time off_____

Time on_____

Total time_____

1. List the customer concern:

2. Research the particular concern in the appropriate service manual.
   a. List the possible causes:

3. Inspect the steering and suspension system to determine the cause of the concern. List the steps you took to determine the fault:

4. List the cause of the concern:

5. List the necessary action/s to correct this fault:

6. Have your supervisor/instructor verify satisfactory completion of this procedure, any observations found, and any necessary action/s recommended.

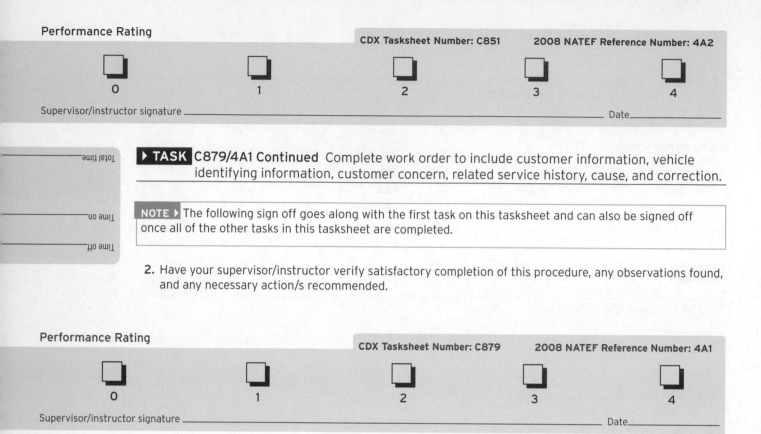

Performance Rating

CDX Tasksheet Number: C851   2008 NATEF Reference Number: 4A2

0   1   2   3   4

Supervisor/instructor signature _____ Date_____

Total time

Time on

Time off

▶ **TASK** **C879/4A1 Continued** Complete work order to include customer information, vehicle identifying information, customer concern, related service history, cause, and correction.

NOTE ▶ The following sign off goes along with the first task on this tasksheet and can also be signed off once all of the other tasks in this tasksheet are completed.

2. Have your supervisor/instructor verify satisfactory completion of this procedure, any observations found, and any necessary action/s recommended.

Performance Rating

CDX Tasksheet Number: C879   2008 NATEF Reference Number: 4A1

0   1   2   3   4

Supervisor/instructor signature _____ Date_____

Wheel and Tire Maintenance

Student/intern information:

Name_____ Date_____ Class_____

Vehicle used for this activity:

Year_____ Make_____ Model_____

Odometer_____ VIN _____

Time off_____

Time on_____

Total time_____

Learning Objective/Task	CDX Tasksheet Number	2008 NATEF Reference Number	2008 NATEF Priority Level
• Inspect tire condition; identify tire wear patterns; check and adjust air pressure; determine necessary action.	C619	4F1	P-1
• Rotate tires according to manufacturer's recommendations.	C222	4F3	P-1
• Reinstall wheel; torque lug nuts.	C227	4F8	P-1
• Dismount, inspect, and remount tire on wheel; balance wheel and tire assembly (static and dynamic).	C620	4F6	P-1
• Dismount, inspect, and remount tire on wheel equipped with tire pressure monitoring system sensor.	C621	4F7	P-2

Recommended Resource Materials

- CDX Automotive program
- Technical service bulletins, shop manuals, and any other information applicable to the specific vehicle or components you are working on
- Class notes

Materials Required

- Worn tire assigned by supervisor/instructor
- Tread depth gauge
- Tire pressure gauge
- Tire inflator
- Vehicle hoist
- Lug wrench (or impact wrench with appropriate impact socket)
- Torque wrench and appropriate socket
- Tire mounting and balancing equipment
- Depending on the type of concern, special diagnostic tools may be required. See your supervisor/instructor for instructions to identify what tools may be required.

Some Safety Issues to Consider

- Worn or damaged tires may have steel cords sticking out of the tire. These wires are very sharp and will severely cut you. Do not rub your hand across a tire without checking first for exposed cords.
- Vehicle hoists are important tools that increase productivity and make the job easier. However, they also can cause severe injury or death if used improperly. Make sure you follow the hoist and vehicle manufacturer's operation procedures.
- Compressed air can be very dangerous. Never blow it at someone. Never use it to remove dirt or dust from your skin or clothing. Never use it without an OSHA-approved nozzle.
- Over-inflating tires could cause the tire to explode with great force. Never exceed the maximum tire pressure for the tire you are working on.
- Lug nuts must always be torqued to the proper torque. Always use a properly calibrated torque wrench. Never use an impact wrench to tighten lug nuts. This could cause the wheel to come loose and fall off if undertightened. Or, if overtightened, the lug studs might get damaged which could also cause the wheel to fall off the vehicle. It could also cause the brake rotors to become warped.

- Always wear the correct protective eyewear and clothing and use the appropriate safety equipment, as well as fender covers, seat protectors, and floor mat protectors.
- Make sure you understand and observe all legislative and personal safety procedures when carrying out practical assignments. If you are unsure of what these are, ask your supervisor/instructor.

Performance Standard

0–No exposure: No information or practice provided during the program; complete training required
1–Exposure only: General information provided with no practice time; close supervision needed; additional training required
2–Limited practice: Has practiced job during training program; additional training required to develop skill
3–Moderately skilled: Has performed job independently during training program; limited additional training may be required
4–Skilled: Can perform job independently with no additional training

Total time _____

Time on _____

Time off _____

▶ **TASK** Inspect tire condition; identify tire wear patterns; check and adjust air pressure; determine necessary action. C619 4F1

1. Research tread wear patterns in the appropriate manual.
2. Research the following specifications on the vehicle's tire decal and on the tire itself:
   a. Tire decal (usually located on the vehicle door, door pillar, or glove box lid):
      i.   Recommended tire designation: _____
      ii. Recommended tire pressure: Front: _____ psi/kPa
           Rear: _____ psi/kPa
   b. Information on sidewall of tire:
      i.   Tire designation: _____
      ii. Maximum pressure: _____ psi/kPa
      iii. Tread wear rating: _____
      iv. Traction rating: _____
      v.   Temperature rating: _____
3. Measure the tread depth across the tire tread and list your measurements below:
   a. Tread depth (inside of tread): _____ in/mm
   b. Tread depth (center of tread): _____ in/mm
   c. Tread depth (outside of tread): _____ in/mm
4. Check to make sure there are no exposed steel cords. Carefully run your hand across the tread and feel for a feathered condition. Also, run your hand in line with the tread to feel for lumps and bulges.
   a. Is the tire feathered? **Yes/No** (Circle one)
   b. Are there any bulges? **Yes/No** (Circle one)
5. Based on your observations and measurements, determine what, if any, wear patterns exist and list them here:

6. Measure the pressure in this tire/s and record it here: _____ psi/kPa
7. If the tire is not at the correct pressure, add or remove pressure.
   a. Record final pressure: _____ psi/kPa
8. Determine any necessary action/s:

9. Have your supervisor/instructor verify satisfactory completion of this procedure, any observations found, and any necessary action/s recommended.

Performance Rating

CDX Tasksheet Number: C619   2008 NATEF Reference Number: 4F1

☐   ☐   ☐   ☐   ☐

0   1   2   3   4

Supervisor/instructor signature _____ Date_____

▶ **TASK** Rotate tires according to manufacturer's recommendations.   **C222 4F3**

Time off_____

Time on_____

NOTE ▶ Vehicles equipped with a tire pressure monitoring system (TPMS) may need the system reset after rotating the tires. Verify that you have all the necessary tools and manufacturer's procedure prior to removing the wheels on these vehicles.

Total time_____

1. Research the following specifications in an appropriate manual.
   a. Is this vehicle equipped with TPMS? **Yes/No** (Circle one)
      i. If yes, do you have the specified tools and procedures to reset this? **Yes/No** (Circle one)
   b. Lug nut torque: _____ ft-lbs/Nm
   c. Manufacturer's recommended tire rotation pattern. Draw diagram below:

   d. Manufacturer's recommended lug nut torque sequence. Draw diagram below.

2. Remove the wheel/tire assemblies from the vehicle.

NOTE ▶ When removing hub caps and wheels, please store them in such a manner as not to damage the visible side of the hub cap or wheel. Laying them face down will cause them to become scratched and damaged. Also, store the lug nuts so they will not get lost or kicked.

3. Have your supervisor/instructor verify removal and initial here:
   a. Supervisor/instructor's initials: _____

4. Rotate the tires according to the manufacturer's recommendation. As part of this procedure, check the tire pressure. If a tire is found to be under-inflated, check the tire for a leak. If a leak is found, notify your supervisor/instructor for further directions. Also, inspect each tire for nails or other foreign objects. Notify your supervisor/instructor if a problem is found. List your observations:

5. Torque the lug nuts to manufacturer's specifications in the specified sequence.
   a. Record torque: _____ ft-lbs/Nm

6. Reset TPMS if necessary. Follow manufacturer's procedure.

7. Reinstall hub caps, if equipped. Make sure they are fully seated to prevent them from falling off while driving. If in doubt, ask your supervisor/instructor.

8. Have your supervisor/instructor verify satisfactory completion of this procedure, any observations found, and any necessary action/s recommended.

▶ **TASK** Reinstall wheel; torque lug nuts.   C227 4F8

NOTE ▶ The above task also satisfies the requirements for task **C227: Reinstall wheel; torque lug nuts.** Have your instructor sign off this task at the same time.

Total time

Time on

Time off

▶ **TASK** Dismount, inspect, and remount tire on wheel; balance wheel and tire assembly (static and dynamic).   C620 4F6

NOTE ▶ Verify that this wheel is not equipped with TPMS.

1. List the customer concern, if any:

2. Prepare the vehicle and remove the wheel concerned.
3. Inspect the outside of the tire and wheel and list your observations:

4. Using the correct procedure, dismount the tire from the wheel.
5. Inspect the inside of the tire, the tire bead, the inside of the rim, and the valve stem. List your observations:

6. Have your supervisor/instructor verify removal and initial here:
   a. Supervisor/instructor's initials: _____

7. Remount tire on wheel using the correct equipment and procedure.

8. Balance wheel and tire assembly (static and dynamic) and record your results:

9. Determine any necessary action/s:

10. Have your supervisor/instructor verify satisfactory completion of this procedure, any observations found, and any necessary action/s recommended.

Performance Rating

CDX Tasksheet Number: C620   2008 NATEF Reference Number: 4F6

☐	☐	☐	☐	☐
0	1	2	3	4

Supervisor/instructor signature _____ Date_____

▶ **TASK** Dismount, inspect, and remount tire on wheel equipped with tire pressure monitoring system sensor.   C621 4F7

Time off_____

Time on_____

Vehicle used for this activity:

Year_____ Make_____ Model_____

Odometer_____ VIN _____

Total time_____

1. List the customer concern, if any:

2. Research the following in the appropriate service information:
   a. Tire removal/installation on TPMS equipped vehicles
   b. TPMS maintenance needs and service
   c. TPMS reset procedure, if necessary

3. Prepare the vehicle and remove the wheel concerned.

4. Inspect the outside of the tire and wheel and list your observations:

5. Using the correct procedure, dismount the tire from the wheel. Be careful not to damage the TPMS sensor.

6. Inspect the inside of the tire, the tire bead, the inside of the rim, the valve stem, and TPMS sensor. List your observations:

7. Have your supervisor/instructor verify removal and initial here:
   a. Supervisor/instructor's initials: _____

8. Perform any needed maintenance/service on the TPMS system.

9. Remount tire on wheel using the correct equipment and procedure. Be careful not to damage the TPMS sensor.

10. Balance wheel and tire assembly, if necessary, and record your results:

11. Reinstall wheel/tire assembly on the vehicle and torque lug nuts to the proper torque.

12. Reset the TPMS according to the manufacturer's procedure.

13. Determine any necessary action/s:

14. Have your supervisor/instructor verify satisfactory completion of this procedure, any observations found, and any necessary action/s recommended.

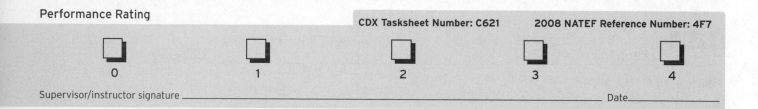

Performance Rating

CDX Tasksheet Number: C621   **2008 NATEF Reference Number: 4F7**

☐ 0   ☐ 1   ☐ 2   ☐ 3   ☐ 4

Supervisor/instructor signature _____ Date_____

Wheel and Tire Diagnosis

Student/intern information:

Name_____ Date_____ Class_____

Vehicle used for this activity:

Year_____ Make_____ Model_____

Odometer_____ VIN _____

Learning Objective/Task	CDX Tasksheet Number	2008 NATEF Reference Number	2008 NATEF Priority Level
• Inspect tire and wheel assembly for air loss; perform necessary action.	C580	4F9	P-1
• Repair tire using internal patch.	C552	4F10	P-1
• Inspect, diagnose, and calibrate tire pressure monitoring system.	C553	4F11	P-2
• Measure wheel, tire, axle flange, and hub runout; determine necessary action.	C701	4F4	P-2
• Diagnose wheel/tire vibration, shimmy, and noise; determine necessary action.	C855	4F2	P-2
• Diagnose tire pull problems; determine necessary action.	C796	4F5	P-2

Time off_____

Time on_____

Total time_____

Recommended Resource Materials

- CDX Automotive program
- Technical service bulletins, shop manuals, and any other information applicable to the specific vehicle or components you are working on
- Class notes

Materials Required

- Leaky tire assigned by supervisor/instructor
- Tire pressure gauge
- Tire inflator
- Vehicle hoist or floor jack and jack stand/s
- Lug wrench (or impact wrench with appropriate impact socket)
- Tire dunk tank or soapy water in a spray bottle
- Torque wrench and appropriate socket
- Tire patching tools and supplies
- Dial indicator
- Depending on the type of concern, special diagnostic tools may be required. See your supervisor/instructor for instructions to identify what tools may be required.

Some Safety Issues to Consider

- Worn or damaged tires may have steel cords sticking out of the tire. These wires are very sharp and will severely cut you. Do not rub your hand across a tire without checking first for exposed cords.
- Vehicle hoists are important tools that increase productivity and make the job easier. However, they also can cause severe injury or death if used improperly. Make sure you follow the hoist and vehicle manufacturer's operation procedures.
- Compressed air can be very dangerous. Never blow it at someone. Never use it to remove dirt or dust from your skin or clothing. Never use it without an OSHA-approved nozzle.
- Over-inflating tires could cause the tire to explode with great force. Never exceed the maximum tire pressure for the tire you are working on.

- Lug nuts must always be torqued to the proper torque. Always use a properly calibrated torque wrench. Never use an impact wrench to tighten lug nuts. This could cause the wheel to come loose and fall off if undertightened. Or, if overtightened, the lug studs might get damaged which could also cause the wheel to fall off the vehicle. It could also cause the brake rotors to become warped.
- Always wear the correct protective eyewear and clothing and use the appropriate safety equipment, as well as fender covers, seat protectors, and floor mat protectors.
- Make sure you understand and observe all legislative and personal safety procedures when carrying out practical assignments. If you are unsure of what these are, ask your supervisor/instructor.

Performance Standard

0–No exposure: No information or practice provided during the program; complete training required
1–Exposure only: General information provided with no practice time; close supervision needed; additional training required
2–Limited practice: Has practiced job during training program; additional training required to develop skill
3–Moderately skilled: Has performed job independently during training program; limited additional training may be required
4–Skilled: Can perform job independently with no additional training

▶ **TASK** Inspect tire and wheel assembly for air loss; perform necessary action.   `C580 4F9`

1. Research the following specifications in an appropriate manual.
   a. Lug nut torque: _____ ft-lbs/Nm
   b. Is this vehicle equipped with TPMS? **Yes/No** (Circle one)
   c. If yes, do you have the specified tools and procedures to reset this? **Yes/No** (Circle one)
2. Remove wheel/tire assembly from vehicle and check it for any leaks using soapy water or a dunk tank. List your observations:

> **NOTE** ▶ When removing hub caps and wheels, please store them in such a manner as not to damage the visible side of the hub cap or wheel. Laying them face down will cause them to become scratched and damaged. Also store the lug nuts so they will not get lost or kicked.

3. Mark the position of all wheel weights and the valve stem on the tire with a tire crayon. This is so you can reinstall the tire and weights on the wheel in the same position so rebalancing is unnecessary.
4. Using the correct procedure, dismount the tire from the wheel. Be careful not to damage the TPMS, if equipped.
5. Inspect the wheel and tire for any damage, rust, or other defects and list them here:

6. Are the defects repairable? **Yes/No** (Circle one)
7. Have your supervisor/instructor verify your observations, and ask permission to make any repairs.
   a. Supervisor/instructor initials: _____
8. With supervisor/instructor approval, repair all defects found.

> **NOTE** ▶ If the tire has a leak which can be repaired with an internal patch, skip ahead to task **C552: Repair tire using internal patch** and return here once the task has been completed.

9. Remount the tire on the wheel, positioning the tire and weights in their original positions on the wheel to restore existing tire balance.
10. Recheck the wheel/tire assembly for leaks. If there are none, reinstall it on the vehicle and torque the lug nuts to the proper specification and in the proper sequence.

11. Have your supervisor/instructor verify satisfactory completion of this procedure, any observations found, and any necessary action/s recommended.

▶ **TASK** Repair tire using internal patch.   C552 4F10

Time off_____

Time on_____

1. Inspect the tire for remaining tread life and ensure that any repair undertaken will meet all legislative requirements.
   a. Measure the minimum tread depth: _____ in/mm
   b. Is the tread depth above the legal limit? **Yes/No** (Circle one)
   c. Is the hole within the repairable zone of the tread? **Yes/No** (Circle one)
2. Using a recommended method, prepare the tire for repair. List your observations here:

Total time_____

3. Determine any necessary action/s, and undertake the repair by applying the patch in accordance with the manufacturer's recommendations and process.
4. Have your supervisor/instructor verify satisfactory completion of this procedure, any observations found, and any necessary action/s recommended.

▶ **TASK** Inspect, diagnose, and calibrate tire pressure monitoring system.   C553 4F11

Time off_____

Time on_____

Vehicle used for this activity:

Year_____ Make_____ Model_____

Odometer_____ VIN _____

Total time_____

1. List the customer concern:

2. Research the particular concern in the appropriate service manual.
   a. List the possible causes:

b. List, or print off and attach to this sheet, the procedure for diagnosing the concern:

3. Inspect, diagnose any potential faults, and calibrate tire pressure monitoring system in accordance with the manufacturer's instructions. List your observations here:

4. List the cause of the concern:

5. Determine any necessary action/s to correct the fault:

6. Have your supervisor/instructor verify satisfactory completion of this procedure, any observations found, and any necessary action/s recommended.

Performance Rating

CDX Tasksheet Number: C553   **2008 NATEF Reference Number: 4F11**

□	□	□	□	□
0	1	2	3	4

Supervisor/instructor signature _____ Date_____

Total time

Time on

Time off

▶ **TASK** Measure wheel, tire, axle flange, and hub runout; determine necessary action.

C701 4F4

Vehicle used for this activity:

Year_____ Make_____ Model_____

Odometer_____ VIN _____

1. List the customer concern:

2. Research the procedure for measuring tire, wheel, and hub runout in the appropriate service information. List the following specifications:
   a. Tire pressure: _____ psi/kPa
   b. Tire designation: _____
   c. Maximum tire runout: _____ in/mm
   d. Maximum wheel runout: _____ in/mm
   e. Maximum axle flange/hub runout: _____ in/mm

3. Check and adjust the tire pressures according to specifications.

4. Inspect each tire and list its designation:

   a. LF: _____

   b. RF: _____

   c. RR: _____

   d. LR: _____

   e. Does each tire meet the manufacturer's recommendations? **Yes/No** (Circle one)

5. Properly raise the front of the vehicle and support it securely.

6. Following the manufacturer's procedure, measure runout of the following:

   a. LF tire: _____ in/mm

   b. RF tire: _____ in/mm

   c. LF wheel: _____ in/mm

   d. RF wheel: _____ in/mm

   e. LF hub: _____ in/mm

   f. RF hub: _____ in/mm

7. Determine any necessary action/s:

8. Have your supervisor/instructor verify satisfactory completion of this procedure, any observations found, and any necessary action/s recommended.

Performance Rating

CDX Tasksheet Number: C701   2008 NATEF Reference Number: 4F4

☐ 0   ☐ 1   ☐ 2   ☐ 3   ☐ 4

Supervisor/instructor signature _____ Date_____

▶ **TASK** Diagnose wheel/tire vibration, shimmy, and noise; determine necessary action.   C855 4F2

Time off_____

Time on_____

Vehicle used for this activity:

Year_____ Make_____ Model_____

Odometer_____ VIN _____

Total time_____

1. List the wheel/tire-related customer concern/s:

2. Research the concern in the appropriate service manual and any technical service bulletins that may apply.

   a. List any applicable service bulletins:

   b. List, or print off and attach to this sheet, the procedure for diagnosing the concern:

3. With the supervisor/instructor's permission, test drive the vehicle. Listen and feel for any unusual noises and vibrations. List your observations:

4. Using the recommended procedure, inspect and diagnose any vibration, shimmy, or noise concerns. List your tests and results here:

5. List the cause of the concern:

6. Determine any necessary action/s to correct the fault:

7. Have your supervisor/instructor verify satisfactory completion of this procedure, any observations found, and any necessary action/s recommended.

Performance Rating

CDX Tasksheet Number: C855   **2008 NATEF Reference Number: 4F2**

☐	☐	☐	☐	☐
0	1	2	3	4

Supervisor/instructor signature _____ Date_____

Total time

Time on

Time off

▶ **TASK** Diagnose tire pull problems; determine necessary action. _____ C796 4F5

Vehicle used for this activity:

Year_____ Make_____ Model_____

Odometer_____ VIN _____

1. List the tire pull-related customer concern/s:

2. Research the configuration of this vehicle in the appropriate service manual and any technical service bulletins that may apply.
   a. List any applicable service bulletins:

b. List, or print off and attach to this sheet, the procedure for diagnosing the concern:

3. With the supervisor/instructor's permission, test drive the vehicle. Check for any tire pull problems. List your observations:

4. Using the recommended procedure, inspect and diagnose any tire pull problems. List your tests and results here:

5. List the cause of the concern:

6. Determine any necessary action/s to correct the fault:

7. Have your supervisor/instructor verify satisfactory completion of this procedure, any observations found, and any necessary action/s recommended.

Performance Rating

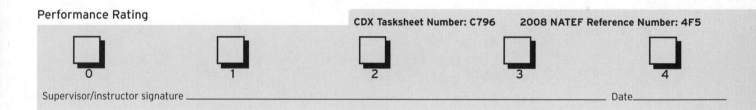

CDX Tasksheet Number: C796   2008 NATEF Reference Number: 4F5

0   1   2   3   4

Supervisor/instructor signature _____ Date_____

Power Steering Pump Maintenance and Service

Student/intern information:

Name_____ Date_____ Class_____

Vehicle used for this activity:

Year_____ Make_____ Model_____

Odometer_____ VIN _____

Time off_____

Time on_____

Total time_____

Learning Objective/Task	CDX Tasksheet Number	2008 NATEF Reference Number	2008 NATEF Priority Level
• Determine proper power steering fluid type; inspect fluid level and condition.	C177	4B10	P-1
• Flush, fill, and bleed power steering system.	C178	4B11	P-2
• Remove, inspect, replace, and adjust power steering pump belt.	C180	4B13	P-1
• Remove and reinstall power steering pump.	C181	4B14	P-2
• Remove and reinstall press fit power steering pump pulley; check pulley and belt alignment.	C699	4B15	P-2
• Inspect and replace power steering hoses and fittings.	C183	4B16	P-2
• Diagnose power steering fluid leakage; determine necessary action.	C179	4B12	P-2

Recommended Resource Materials

- CDX Automotive program
- Technical service bulletins, shop manuals, and any other information applicable to the specific vehicle or components you are working on
- Class notes

Materials Required

- Vehicle or simulator, equipped with power steering
- Correct power steering fluid
- White piece of paper
- Power steering flush machine or drain pan
- Funnel
- Belt tension gauge
- Power steering pump pulley remover/installer tool
- Depending on the type of concern, special diagnostic tools may be required. See your supervisor/instructor for instructions to identify what tools may be required.

Some Safety Issues to Consider

- You will be working under the hood of a running vehicle. Keep your hands and fingers away from moving belts, fans, and other parts.
- When running any vehicles in the shop, make sure you use the shop's exhaust ventilation system to discharge all exhaust gas safely outside.
- Lifting equipment such as vehicle jacks and stands, vehicle hoists, and engine hoists are important tools that increase productivity and make the job easier. But they can also cause severe injury or death if used improperly. Make sure you follow the manufacturer's operation procedures. Also make sure you have your supervisor/instructor's permission to use any particular type of lifting equipment.
- Caution must be exercised when working around the power steering pump, especially if the vehicle has been driven recently or the engine is at operating temperature. The power steering fluid can be extremely hot and can burn if it comes in contact with unprotected skin. When operating the power steering system, it can be under high hydraulic pressure.

- Always wear the correct protective eyewear and clothing and use the appropriate safety equipment, as well as fender covers, seat protectors, and floor mat protectors.
- Make sure you understand and observe all legislative and personal safety procedures when carrying out practical assignments. If you are unsure of what these are, ask your supervisor/instructor.

Performance Standard

0—No exposure: No information or practice provided during the program; complete training required

1—Exposure only: General information provided with no practice time; close supervision needed; additional training required

2—Limited practice: Has practiced job during training program; additional training required to develop skill

3—Moderately skilled: Has performed job independently during training program; limited additional training may be required

4—Skilled: Can perform job independently with no additional training

▶ **TASK** Determine proper power steering fluid type; inspect fluid level and condition.

C177 4B10

1. Research specified power steering fluid for this vehicle using the appropriate service manual.
   a. Specified fluid: _____
   b. When should the fluid be checked? **Hot/Cold/Either** (Circle one)
   c. If the service manual lists a procedure for flushing the power steering fluid, list the main steps (you can paraphrase, or print off the procedure):

2. Follow the manufacturer's procedure to check the fluid level.
3. Locate the power steering fluid reservoir.
   a. List the level of the power steering fluid: _____

NOTE ▶ If power steering fluid is below the minimum level, it could mean there is a leak in the system. Investigate this possibility and report it to your supervisor/instructor.

4. Place a small amount of the fluid from the reservoir on a white piece of paper and describe its condition:

5. Determine any necessary action/s:

6. Have your supervisor/instructor verify satisfactory completion of this procedure, any observations found, and any necessary action/s recommended.

Total time

Time on

Time off

Performance Rating

CDX Tasksheet Number: C177   2008 NATEF Reference Number: 4B10

0	1	2	3	4
☐	☐	☐	☐	☐

Supervisor/instructor signature _____ Date_____

▶ **TASK** Flush, fill, and bleed power steering system.   C178 4B11

Time off_____

Time on_____

Total time_____

1. Follow the service manual to flush the power steering fluid. If no procedure is specified, ask your supervisor/instructor to approve the following procedure: _____
   a. With the engine off, place a drain pan under the power steering pump return hose and out of the way of the fan or other moving parts.
   b. Remove the return hose from the power steering pump. Place the return hose in the drain pan. Plug the return line fitting in the power steering pump with an appropriate plug or cap.
   c. Fill the reservoir to the proper level with new fluid. Have an assistant start the engine and slowly turn the steering wheel to flush out the old fluid. At the same time, continue to add fluid to the reservoir (with the funnel) to keep it approximately full. Continue this until clean fluid comes out of the return line and then turn off the vehicle.
   d. Reinstall the return line and fill the reservoir to the proper level.
   e. Start the vehicle again and turn the steering wheel a few times from lock to lock. Check the fluid level and top off as necessary.
   f. If a buzzing noise is heard, there is probably air trapped in the system. In this case, turn off the engine, raise the front wheels off the ground (support the vehicle on jack stands or a hoist), and turn the wheels from lock to lock with the engine off. Do this several times. Check the fluid level and top off if necessary. Lower the vehicle. Restart the engine and listen and feel for proper operation. Repeat if necessary.
   g. Properly dispose of the old power steering fluid.

2. Have your supervisor/instructor verify satisfactory completion of this procedure, any observations found, and any necessary action/s recommended.

Performance Rating

		CDX Tasksheet Number: C178	2008 NATEF Reference Number: 4B11	
☐	☐	☐	☐	☐
0	1	2	3	4

Supervisor/instructor signature _____ Date_____

▶ **TASK** Remove, inspect, replace, and adjust power steering pump belt.   C180 4B13

Time off_____

Time on_____

Total time_____

1. Using the service information, list the following:
   a. Type of power steering fluid: _____
   b. Type of belt: **V-belt/Serpentine belt/Toothed belt** (Circle one)
   c. Belt adjustment mechanism: **Manual/Automatic** (Circle one)
   d. Belt tension, if specified: _____
   e. Draw, or print off and attach to this sheet, the belt routing diagram:

2. Following the recommended procedure, loosen the adjustment mechanism and remove the power steering pump drive belt.

3. Examine the belt for cracks, splints, frayed surfaces, and distorted configurations (including stretching). Record your observation/s:

4. Examine the drive pulleys for any damage. Record your observation/s:

5. Have your supervisor/instructor verify removal and your observation/s.
   a. Supervisor/instructor's initials: _____

> **NOTE ▶** You may want to skip ahead and perform the next task **C181: Remove and reinstall power steering pump** while you have the belt removed. If so, return to this point when you are ready to reinstall the drive belt.

6. Following the recommended procedure, replace the drive belt.
7. Check the drive belt alignment in relation to the drive pulleys. List your observation/s:

8. Adjust the drive belt tension to the shop manufacturer's specifications (on the manually adjusted system).
   a. Measure the belt tension: _____
9. Check the fluid level in the power steering reservoir. Top off with the proper fluid, if necessary.
10. Start the engine and turn the steering wheel from lock to lock. Check for the following:
    a. Binding: **Yes/No** (Circle one)
    b. Excessive steering effort: **Yes/No** (Circle one)
    c. Uneven steering effort: **Yes/No** (Circle one)
11. Turn the engine off.
12. Re-measure the drive belt tension and list here: _____
13. Have your supervisor/instructor verify satisfactory completion of this procedure, any observations found, and any necessary action/s recommended.

Performance Rating

CDX Tasksheet Number: C180		2008 NATEF Reference Number: 4B13

☐ 0   ☐ 1   ☐ 2   ☐ 3   ☐ 4

Supervisor/instructor signature _____ Date_____

Total time

Time on

Time off

▶ **TASK** Remove and reinstall power steering pump.   C181 4B14

1. Research the procedure to remove and install the power steering pump. List the steps or print off the procedure:

2. Following the service manual procedure, remove the power steering pump being careful not to damage any fittings or hoses. Also, pay close attention to the positioning of any brackets and spacers.
3. Inspect the pump and pulley. List your observation/s:

© Jones and Bartlett Publishers, LLC

4. Have your supervisor/instructor verify removal and your observation/s.
   a. Supervisor/instructor's initials: _____

> **NOTE ▶** You may want to skip ahead and perform the next task **C699: Remove and reinstall press fit power steering pump pulley; check pulley and belt alignment** while you have the pump removed. If so, return to this point when you are ready to reinstall the pump.

5. Following the specified procedure, reinstall the power steering pump. Be careful to properly align all brackets, fittings, and hoses. Also, tighten all fasteners to their specified torque.

> **NOTE ▶** Return to task **C180: Remove, inspect, replace, and adjust power steering pump belt** step 6 to complete that task.

6. Have your supervisor/instructor verify satisfactory completion of this procedure, any observations found, and any necessary action/s recommended.

Performance Rating

		CDX Tasksheet Number: C181	2008 NATEF Reference Number: 4B14	
☐	☐	☐	☐	☐
0	1	2	3	4

Supervisor/instructor signature _____ Date_____

▶ TASK Remove and reinstall press fit power steering pump pulley; check pulley and belt alignment.

C699 4B15

Time off_____

Time on_____

Total time_____

1. Research the procedure to remove and install the power steering pump pulley. List the steps or print off the procedure:

2. Using the appropriate tools, remove the press fit power steering pump drive pulley from the drive shaft and inspect the pulley for any damage. List your observation/s:

3. Inspect the pump drive shaft and shaft seal for any damage. List your observation/s:

4. Have your supervisor/instructor verify removal and your observation/s.
   a. Supervisor/instructor's initials: _____

5. Reinstall the press fit drive pulley on the power steering pump using the appropriate tool/s.

6. Have your supervisor/instructor verify satisfactory completion of this procedure, any observations found, and any necessary action/s recommended.

▶ **TASK** Inspect and replace power steering hoses and fittings.   C183 4B16

1. Research the procedure to remove and install the power steering hoses and fittings. List the steps or print off the procedure:

2. Following the shop manual instructions, drain the power steering fluid into a clean container for proper disposal according to environmental guidelines and regulations.

3. Disconnect power steering hoses from both the power steering pump and the power steering box or rack. Plug any exposed fittings to prevent entry of dirt or debris.

4. Disconnect any retaining clips.

5. Remove power steering hoses from the vehicle and place on your workbench.

6. Examine the flexible hoses for cracks, splits, chafed surfaces, and distorted configurations (including hardening and loss of flexibility). List your observation/s:

7. Examine any steel tubes and fittings, check for heat damage, splits, kinking, damaged threads, or restrictions. List your observation/s:

8. Have your supervisor/instructor verify removal and your observation/s.
   a. Supervisor/instructor's initials: _____

9. Following the specified procedure, reinstall the power steering hoses being careful not to cross-thread any fittings or damage any hoses or tubes.

10. Have your supervisor/instructor verify satisfactory completion of this procedure, any observations found, and any necessary action/s recommended.

NOTE ▶ Return to task **C181: Remove and reinstall power steering pump** step 5 to reinstall the pump.

Vehicle used for this activity:

Year_____ Make_____ Model_____

Odometer_____ VIN _____

> **NOTE ►** If the vehicle's engine assembly is coated with leaking fluids and road dirt, you may need to pressure wash the engine compartment before inspecting for leaks. Get your instructor's permission before performing a cleaning operation.

> **NOTE ►** Some very small leaks, or leaks in engines that have a lot of accumulated residue, may be best diagnosed with the use of a fluorescent dye and ultraviolet light. Check with your instructor if this vehicle is a good candidate for that procedure. If so, follow the dye check equipment manufacturer's instructions for performing this test.

1. Using a good light, inspect under the hood for any power steering fluid leaks. Inspect the reservoir, pump (including shaft seal), hoses, and fittings. List your observation/s:

2. Raise the vehicle safely on the hoist. Inspect the power steering pump, hoses, and gear box for leaks.

> **NOTE ►** Remember that gravity tends to pull any leaking fluid down. You may need to identify the highest point of the leak to locate the source.

3. Identify and list the source/s of any leak/s:

4. Determine necessary action/s:

5. Have your supervisor/instructor verify satisfactory completion of this procedure, any observations found, and any necessary action/s recommended.

Performance Rating

CDX Tasksheet Number: C179   2008 NATEF Reference Number: 4B12

☐	☐	☐	☐	☐
0	1	2	3	4

Supervisor/instructor signature _____ Date_____

Steering Linkage Service

© Jones and Bartlett Publishers, LLC

Student/intern information:

Name_____ Date_____ Class_____

Vehicle used for this activity:

Year_____ Make_____ Model_____

Odometer_____ VIN _____

Learning Objective/Task	CDX Tasksheet Number	2008 NATEF Reference Number	2008 NATEF Priority Level
• Inspect and replace pitman arm, relay (centerlink/intermediate) rod, idler arm and mountings, and steering linkage damper.	C184	4B17	P-2
• Inspect, replace, and adjust tie rod ends (sockets), tie rod sleeves, and clamps.	C185	4B18	P-1

Recommended Resource Materials

- CDX Automotive program
- Technical service bulletins, shop manuals, and any other information applicable to the specific vehicle or components you are working on
- Class notes

Materials Required

- Vehicle hoist
- Vehicle with recirculating ball steering gear system
- Pitman arm puller
- Depending on the type of concern, special diagnostic tools may be required. See your supervisor/instructor for instructions to identify what tools may be required.

Some Safety Issues to Consider

- Lifting equipment such as vehicle jacks and stands, vehicle hoists, and engine hoists are important tools that increase productivity and make the job easier. But they can also cause severe injury or death if used improperly. Make sure you follow the manufacturer's operation procedures. Also, make sure you have your supervisor/instructor's permission to use any particular type of lifting equipment.
- Always wear the correct protective eyewear and clothing and use the appropriate safety equipment, as well as fender covers, seat protectors, and floor mat protectors.
- Make sure you understand and observe all legislative and personal safety procedures when carrying out practical assignments. If you are unsure of what these are, ask your supervisor/instructor.

Performance Standard

0—No exposure: No information or practice provided during the program; complete training required

1—Exposure only: General information provided with no practice time; close supervision needed; additional training required

2—Limited practice: Has practiced job during training program; additional training required to develop skill

3—Moderately skilled: Has performed job independently during training program; limited additional training may be required

4—Skilled: Can perform job independently with no additional training

▶ **TASK** Inspect and replace pitman arm, relay (centerlink/intermediate) rod, idler arm and mountings, and steering linkage damper.   C184 4B17

1. Research the following specifications and procedures in the appropriate service information.
   a. Pitman arm locking nut torque: _____ ft-lbs/Nm
   b. Tie rod nut torque: _____ ft-lbs/Nm
   c. Maximum allowable play in steering linkage joints: _____ in/mm
2. Lift and support the vehicle according to the procedure listed in the service information.

3. Follow the manufacturer's procedure and inspect the steering system parts listed.
   a. Pitman arm. List your observation/s:

   b. Relay (centerlink/intermediate) rod. List your observation/s:

   c. Idler arm and mountings. List your observation/s:

   d. Steering linkage damper, if equipped. List your observation/s:

   e. Tie rod ends. List your observation/s:

   f. Tie rod sleeves and clamps. List your observation/s:

4. Following the manufacturer's procedure, mark the location of the pitman arm shaft and pitman arm splines. Disconnect the pitman arm from the relay (centerlink/intermediate) rod steering linkage.
5. Remove the pitman arm retaining nut and, using the manufacturer's recommended removal tool, remove the pitman arm.
6. If the vehicle is fitted with a steering damper, remove the steering damper and place it on your workbench.
7. Loosen the tie rod clamps.
8. Remove the relay (centerlink/intermediate) rod steering linkage.

NOTE ▶ The use of a pickle fork will damage the dust boots. Only use this tool on joints you will be replacing. On joints you will be reusing, try the hammer method to break the joint free. See your instructor for details.

9. Remove idler arm assembly.
10. Remove tie rod ends from steering knuckles.
11. Remove tie rod ends from sleeves.

NOTE ▶ Count the number of turns as you back out each tie rod from its sleeve so you can reinstall it in approximately the same position. This will assist in making the wheel alignment easier to perform.

12. Inspect all components and list your observations:

13. Have your supervisor/instructor verify removal and your observations.
    a. Supervisor/instructor's initials: _____

14. Reassemble all components following the manufacturer's recommended procedure, being sure to torque all fasteners and secure all joints with new cotter pins (or other approved method).
    a. List the torque you tightened the pitman arm lock nut: _____ ft-lbs/Nms
    b. Were there other components that needed torquing? If so, list them:

    c. Did you replace all removed cotter pins with new cotter pins? **Yes/No** (Circle one)

15. Start the vehicle and check for binding or improper steering operation. List your observations:

> **NOTE ▸** Before this vehicle can be driven, it MUST have a wheel alignment performed. Failure to do so means this is an unsafe vehicle which could result in substantial injury or even death.

16. Have your supervisor/instructor verify satisfactory completion of this procedure, any observations found, and any necessary action/s recommended.

Performance Rating

		CDX Tasksheet Number: C184	2008 NATEF Reference Number: 4B17	
☐	☐	☐	☐	☐
0	1	2	3	4

Supervisor/instructor signature _____ Date_____

▸ TASK Inspect, replace, and adjust tie rod ends (sockets), tie rod sleeves, and clamps.

C185 4B18

> **NOTE ▸** Completion of the above task also satisfies task **C185: Inspect, replace, and adjust tie rod ends (sockets), tie rod sleeves, and clamps.** Have your instructor sign off this task at the same time.

Performance Rating

		CDX Tasksheet Number: C185	2008 NATEF Reference Number: 4B18	
☐	☐	☐	☐	☐
0	1	2	3	4

Supervisor/instructor signature _____ Date_____

Steering Gear Service

Student/intern information:

Name_____ Date_____ Class_____

Vehicle used for this activity:

Year_____ Make_____ Model_____

Odometer_____ VIN _____

Learning Objective/Task	CDX Tasksheet Number	2008 NATEF Reference Number	2008 NATEF Priority Level
• Remove and replace rack and pinion steering gear; inspect mounting bushings and brackets.	C882	4B8	P-2
• Inspect and replace rack and pinion steering gear inner tie rod ends (sockets) and bellows boots.	C883	4B9	P-2
• Adjust non-rack and pinion worm bearing preload and sector lash.	C881	4B7	P-3

Time off_____

Time on_____

Total time_____

Recommended Resource Materials

- CDX Automotive program
- Technical service bulletins, shop manuals, and any other information applicable to the specific vehicle or components you are working on
- Class notes

Materials Required

- Vehicle hoist
- Vehicle with rack and pinion steering gear system
- Vehicle with non-rack and pinion steering gear system
- Depending on the type of concern, special diagnostic tools may be required. See your supervisor/instructor for instructions to identify what tools may be required.

Some Safety Issues to Consider

- Lifting equipment such as vehicle jacks and stands, vehicle hoists, and engine hoists are important tools that increase productivity and make the job easier. But they can also cause severe injury or death if used improperly. Make sure you follow the manufacturer's operation procedures. Also, make sure you have your supervisor/instructor's permission to use any particular type of lifting equipment.
- Always wear the correct protective eyewear and clothing and use the appropriate safety equipment, as well as fender covers, seat protectors, and floor mat protectors.
- Make sure you understand and observe all legislative and personal safety procedures when carrying out practical assignments. If you are unsure of what these are, ask your supervisor/instructor.

Performance Standard

0–No exposure: No information or practice provided during the program; complete training required

1–Exposure only: General information provided with no practice time; close supervision needed; additional training required

2–Limited practice: Has practiced job during training program; additional training required to develop skill

3–Moderately skilled: Has performed job independently during training program; limited additional training may be required

4–Skilled: Can perform job independently with no additional training

▶ **TASK** Remove and replace rack and pinion steering gear; inspect mounting bushings and brackets.

C882 4B8

1. Research the following procedures and specifications in the appropriate service information.
   a. R & R rack and pinion flat rate time: _____ hrs
   b. R & R inner tie rod end (either side) flat rate time: _____ hrs
   c. Type of power steering fluid: _____
   d. Rack and pinion steering gear removal. List the main steps (you can paraphrase or print off the procedure):

2. Start the engine and straighten the wheels. Turn the engine off and lock the steering column. This will keep the clock spring centered.

3. Follow the service information procedure to remove the rack and pinion steering gear. Be careful not to damage any lines, tubes, or fittings. Plug any lines or fittings to prevent entry of dirt or debris.

4. Inspect the condition of the mounting bushings and brackets. List your observations:

NOTE ▶ You may want to skip down to task **C883: Inspect and replace rack and pinion steering gear inner tie rod ends (sockets) and bellows boots.** This task will be much easier to perform with the rack and pinion removed from the vehicle. If so, return to this point when you are ready to reinstall the rack and pinion.

5. Follow the service information procedure to reinstall the rack and pinion steering gear. Be careful not to damage any lines, tubes, or fittings. Also, unless the manufacturer directs otherwise, make sure the rack is centered in its travel so that the clock spring will be indexed to the rack.

6. Torque all fasteners and fittings.

7. Check the fluid level in the power steering reservoir. Top off with the proper fluid.

8. Start the engine and bleed any air from the power steering system. Top off fluid as necessary.

9. With the engine running, turn the steering wheel from lock to lock. Check for the following:
   a. Binding: **Yes/No** (Circle one)
   b. Excessive steering effort: **Yes/No** (Circle one)
   c. Uneven steering effort: **Yes/No** (Circle one)

10. Have your supervisor/instructor verify satisfactory completion of this procedure, any observations found, and any necessary action/s recommended.

Performance Rating

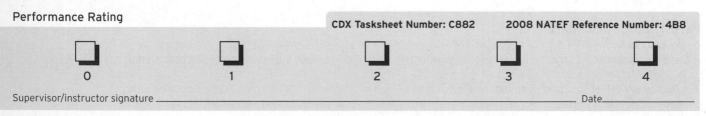

CDX Tasksheet Number: C882   2008 NATEF Reference Number: 4B8

0	1	2	3	4

Supervisor/instructor signature _____ Date_____

© Jones and Bartlett Publishers, LLC

▶ **TASK** Inspect and replace rack and pinion steering gear inner tie rod ends (sockets) and bellows boots. C883 4B9

Time off_____

Time on_____

Total time_____

1. Following the service information procedure, inspect the tie rod ends (sockets) and bellows boots. List your observation/s:

2. Determine which inner tie rod end your supervisor/instructor would like you to remove:
   _____

3. Remove the bellows boot to gain access to the inner tie rod.

4. Following the service information procedure, extend the rack (by turning the pinion shaft) to expose the locking nut of the inner tie rod socket. Using the appropriate tools, loosen the inner tie rod socket and unscrew the tie rod end.

5. Inspect the components and list your observations:

6. Have your supervisor/instructor verify removal and your observation/s.
   a. Supervisor/instructor's initials: _____

7. Following the service information procedure, reassemble the inner tie rod socket and torque to the manufacturer's specifications.

8. Have your supervisor/instructor verify proper torque.
   a. Supervisor/instructor's initials: _____

9. Reassemble the bellows boot and secure it according to the manufacturer's procedure.

10. Have your supervisor/instructor verify satisfactory completion of this procedure, any observations found, and any necessary action/s recommended.

Performance Rating

CDX Tasksheet Number: C883   2008 NATEF Reference Number: 4B9

☐	☐	☐	☐	☐
0	1	2	3	4

Supervisor/instructor signature _____ Date_____

▶ **TASK** Adjust non-rack and pinion worm bearing preload and sector lash. C881 4B7

Time off_____

Time on_____

Total time_____

Vehicle used for this activity:

Year_____ Make_____ Model_____

Odometer_____ VIN _____

1. Research the following procedures and specifications in the appropriate service information.
   a. Worm bearing preload adjustment (paraphrase or print off procedure):

   b. Sector lash adjustment (paraphrase or print off procedure):

2. Following the service information procedure, adjust the worm bearing preload. List your observation/s:

3. Have your supervisor/instructor verify adjustment and your observation/s.
   a. Supervisor/instructor's initials: _____

4. Following the service information procedure, adjust the sector lash. List your observation/s:

5. Have your supervisor/instructor verify adjustment and your observation/s.
   a. Supervisor/instructor's initials: _____

6. Reassemble any removed parts and check steering for proper operation.

7. Have your supervisor/instructor verify satisfactory completion of this procedure, any observations found, and any necessary action/s recommended.

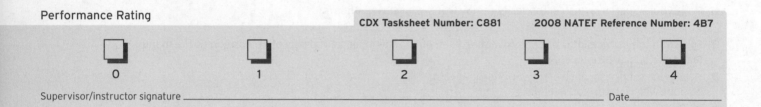

Performance Rating

CDX Tasksheet Number: C881   2008 NATEF Reference Number: 4B7

0   1   2   3   4

Supervisor/instructor signature _____ Date_____

Steering Gear Diagnosis

Student/intern information:

Name_____ Date_____ Class_____

Vehicle used for this activity:

Year_____ Make_____ Model_____

Odometer_____ VIN _____

Learning Objective/Task	CDX Tasksheet Number	2008 NATEF Reference Number	2008 NATEF Priority Level
• Diagnose power steering gear (non-rack and pinion) binding, uneven turning effort, looseness, hard steering, and noise concerns; determine necessary action.	C884	4B4	P-2
• Diagnose power steering gear (rack and pinion) binding, uneven turning effort, looseness, hard steering, and noise concerns; determine necessary action.	C880	4B5	P-2

Time off_____

Time on_____

Total time_____

Recommended Resource Materials

- CDX Automotive program
- Technical service bulletins, shop manuals, and any other information applicable to the specific vehicle or components you are working on
- Class notes

Materials Required

- Vehicle hoist
- Vehicle with rack and pinion steering gear system concern
- Vehicle with non-rack and pinion steering gear system concern
- Depending on the type of concern, special diagnostic tools may be required. See your supervisor/instructor for instructions to identify what tools may be required.

Some Safety Issues to Consider

- Diagnosis of this fault may require test driving the vehicle on the school grounds. Attempt this task only with full permission from your instructor and follow all the guidelines exactly.
- You will be working under the hood of a running vehicle. Keep your hands and fingers away from moving belts, fans, and other parts.
- When running any vehicles in the shop, make sure you use the shop's exhaust ventilation system to discharge all exhaust gas safely outside.
- Lifting equipment such as vehicle jacks and stands, vehicle hoists, and engine hoists are important tools that increase productivity and make the job easier. But they can also cause severe injury or death if used improperly. Make sure you follow the manufacturer's operation procedures. Also, make sure you have your supervisor/instructor's permission to use any particular type of lifting equipment.
- Always wear the correct protective eyewear and clothing and use the appropriate safety equipment, as well as fender covers, seat protectors, and floor mat protectors.
- Make sure you understand and observe all legislative and personal safety procedures when carrying out practical assignments. If you are unsure of what these are, ask your supervisor/instructor.

Performance Standard

0—No exposure: No information or practice provided during the program; complete training required

1—Exposure only: General information provided with no practice time; close supervision needed; additional training required

2—Limited practice: Has practiced job during training program; additional training required to develop skill

3—Moderately skilled: Has performed job independently during training program; limited additional training may be required

4—Skilled: Can perform job independently with no additional training

▶ **TASK** Diagnose power steering gear (non-rack and pinion) binding, uneven turning effort, looseness, hard steering, and noise concerns; determine necessary action.

C884 4B4

1. List the power steering system-related customer concern:

2. Verify the concern and list your observations here:

3. Research the possible causes for this concern in the appropriate service manual.
   a. List, or print off and attach to this sheet, the possible causes:

   b. List, or print off and attach to this sheet, the procedure for diagnosing the concern:

4. Follow the service manual procedure to diagnose the concern. List your tests and results here:

5. List the cause of the concern:

6. Determine any necessary action/s to correct the fault:

7. Have your supervisor/instructor verify satisfactory completion of this procedure, any observations found, and any necessary action/s recommended.

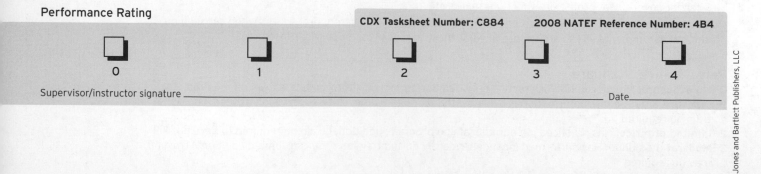

Performance Rating

CDX Tasksheet Number: C884   2008 NATEF Reference Number: 4B4

☐   ☐   ☐   ☐   ☐

0   1   2   3   4

Supervisor/instructor signature _____ Date_____

▶ **TASK** Diagnose power steering gear (rack and pinion) binding, uneven turning effort, looseness, hard steering, and noise concerns; determine necessary action.

C880 4B5

Time off_____

Time on_____

Total time_____

Vehicle used for this activity:

Year_____ Make_____ Model_____

Odometer_____ VIN _____

1. List the power steering system-related customer concern:

2. Verify the concern and list your observations here:

3. Research the possible causes for this concern in the appropriate service manual.
   a. List, or print off and attach to this sheet, the possible causes:

   b. List, or print off and attach to this sheet, the procedure for diagnosing the concern:

4. Follow the service manual procedure to diagnose the concern. List your tests and results here:

5. List the cause of the concern:

6. Determine any necessary action/s to correct the fault:

7. Have your supervisor/instructor verify satisfactory completion of this procedure, any observations found, and any necessary action/s recommended.

Performance Rating

CDX Tasksheet Number: C880   2008 NATEF Reference Number: 4B5

☐	☐	☐	☐	☐
0	1	2	3	4

Supervisor/instructor signature _____ Date_____

Steering Column Service

Student/intern information:

Name_____ Date_____ Class_____

Vehicle used for this activity:

Year_____ Make_____ Model_____

Odometer_____ VIN _____

Time off_____

Time on_____

Total time_____

Learning Objective/Task	CDX Tasksheet Number	2008 NATEF Reference Number	2008 NATEF Priority Level
• Disable and enable supplemental restraint system (SRS).	C168	4B1	P-1
• Remove and replace steering wheel; center/time supplemental restraint system (SRS) coil (clock spring).	C169	4B2	P-1
• Inspect steering shaft universal-joint(s), flexible coupling(s), collapsible column, lock cylinder mechanism, and steering wheel; perform necessary action.	C173	4B6	P-2
• Diagnose steering column noises, looseness, and binding concerns (including tilt mechanisms); determine necessary action.	C170	4B3	P-2

Recommended Resource Materials

- CDX Automotive program
- Technical service bulletins, shop manuals, and any other information applicable to the specific vehicle or components you are working on
- Class notes

Materials Required

- Vehicle fitted with supplemental restraint system (SRS)
- Steering wheel puller
- Manufacturer- and job-specific tools
- Masking tape

Some Safety Issues to Consider

- Working on the airbag system can be very dangerous. Consult the shop manual for the vehicle you are working on and ensure all safety precautions are followed.
- Accidental deployment of the airbag system could happen if you inadvertently probe the wrong wire. Most manufacturers use yellow colored wiring to denote wiring for the airbag system. Always be aware of the system/circuit you are working on.
- Always wear the correct protective eyewear and clothing and use the appropriate safety equipment, as well as fender covers, seat protectors, and floor mat protectors.
- Make sure you understand and observe all legislative and personal safety procedures when carrying out practical assignments. If you are unsure of what these are, ask your supervisor/instructor.

Performance Standard

0–No exposure: No information or practice provided during the program; complete training required

1–Exposure only: General information provided with no practice time; close supervision needed; additional training required

2–Limited practice: Has practiced job during training program; additional training required to develop skill

3–Moderately skilled: Has performed job independently during training program; limited additional training may be required

4–Skilled: Can perform job independently with no additional training

▶ **TASK** Disable and enable supplemental restraint system (SRS).　　C168 4B1

1. Locate "disable vehicle SRS system" in the appropriate service information for the vehicle you are working on.

   a. List, or print off and attach to this sheet, the safety precautions to be taken when disabling the SRS system:

   b. List, or print off and attach to this sheet, the steps to disable the SRS system:

   c. List, or print off and attach to this sheet, the steps to enable the SRS system:

2. Have your supervisor/instructor verify your listed procedures.
   a. Supervisor/instructor initials: _____

3. Disarm the SRS system.

4. Have your supervisor/instructor verify that the SRS is disabled.
   a. Supervisor/instructor initials: _____

> **NOTE ▶** You may want to consider skipping to task **C169: Remove and replace steering wheel; center/time supplemental restraint system (SRS) coil (clock spring)** since it requires disabling the SRS. Return to this step when you complete that task and re-enable the SRS.

5. Enable the vehicle SRS.

6. Have your supervisor/instructor verify satisfactory completion of this procedure, any observations found, and any necessary action/s recommended.

Performance Rating

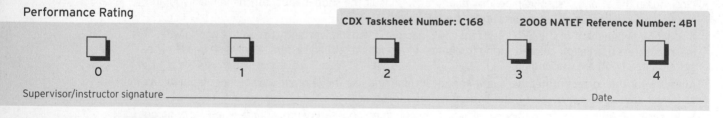

		CDX Tasksheet Number: C168		2008 NATEF Reference Number: 4B1
☐	☐	☐	☐	☐
0	1	2	3	4

Supervisor/instructor signature _____ Date_____

▶ **TASK** Remove and replace steering wheel; center/time supplemental restraint system (SRS) coil (clock spring).　　C169 4B2

1. Locate "remove and replace steering wheel" and "center/time SRS clock spring" procedures in the appropriate service information.

   a. List, or print off and attach to this sheet, the procedures for removing and replacing the steering wheel:

   b. List, or print off and attach to this sheet, the procedure to center/time the SRS clock spring:

2. Have your supervisor/instructor verify your listed procedures.
   a. Supervisor/instructor initials: _____

3. Following the manufacturer's recommended procedures and precautions, remove the steering wheel.

4. Following the manufacturer's recommended procedures and precautions, remove the clock spring.

5. Inspect the components and list your observation/s:

6. Have your supervisor/instructor verify the removal of these components and your observations.
   a. Supervisor/instructor initials: _____

7. Reassemble the steering column. Be sure to follow all manufacturer recommended procedures and precautions.

> **NOTE ▸** Return to task **C168: Disable and enable supplemental restraint system (SRS)** step 5 to enable the SRS.

8. Have your supervisor/instructor verify satisfactory completion of this procedure, any observations found, and any necessary action/s recommended.

Performance Rating

CDX Tasksheet Number: C169   2008 NATEF Reference Number: 4B2

☐   ☐   ☐   ☐   ☐
0   1   2   3   4

Supervisor/instructor signature _____ Date_____

▶ **TASK** Inspect steering shaft universal-joint(s), flexible coupling(s), collapsible column, lock cylinder mechanism, and steering wheel; perform necessary action.   C173 4B6

Time off_____

Time on_____

Total time_____

1. If the vehicle is fitted with a supplemental restraint system (SRS), disable it according to the manufacturer's procedure and precautions.

2. Properly raise and support the vehicle so the tires are a few inches off the floor.

3. With the steering column lock activated, try to turn the steering wheel from side to side.
   a. Is the locking mechanism working? **Yes/No** (Circle one)
   b. List your observation/s here:

4. With the engine ignition key in the "off" position, ensure the steering lock is not engaged and have an assistant rock the steering wheel from side to side (just enough to move the road wheels slightly). While the steering wheel is being rocked, check for any wear or looseness in the shaft universal-joint/s or flexible coupling/s.
   a. List your observation/s here:

5. With reference to the shop manual, check that the steering column collapsible action has not been compromised.
   a. List your observation/s here:

6. Check the steering wheel for the following and list any observation/s:
   a. Looseness on the steering shaft:

   b. Structural damage:

   c. SRS airbag is intact and has appropriate pad/cover:

   d. Size and appropriateness for the make and model of the vehicle (refer to the shop manual):

7. Have your supervisor/instructor verify your observations.
   a. Supervisor/instructor initials: _____
8. Perform any necessary action/s and list them here:

9. Enable the SRS.
10. Have your supervisor/instructor verify satisfactory completion of this procedure, any observations found, and any necessary action/s recommended.

Performance Rating

CDX Tasksheet Number: C173   2008 NATEF Reference Number: 4B6

☐	☐	☐	☐	☐
0	1	2	3	4

Supervisor/instructor signature _____ Date_____

Total time

Time on

Time off

▶ **TASK** Diagnose steering column noises, looseness, and binding concerns (including tilt mechanisms); determine necessary action.

C170 4B3

Vehicle used for this activity:

Year_____ Make_____ Model_____

Odometer_____ VIN _____

1. List the steering column-related customer concern:

2. Verify the concern and list your observations here:

3. Research the possible causes for this concern in the appropriate service manual.
a. List, or print off and attach to this sheet, the possible causes:

b. List, or print off and attach to this sheet, the procedure for diagnosing the concern:

c. List the precautions when working on this steering column:

4. Follow the service manual procedure to diagnose the concern. List your tests and results here:

5. List the cause of the concern:

6. Determine any necessary action/s to correct this fault:

7. Have your supervisor/instructor verify satisfactory completion of this procedure, any observations found, and any necessary action/s recommended.

Performance Rating

CDX Tasksheet Number: C170   **2008 NATEF Reference Number: 4B3**

☐   ☐   ☐   ☐   ☐
0   1   2   3   4

Supervisor/instructor signature _____ Date_____

Student/intern information:

Name_____ Date_____ Class_____

Vehicle used for this activity:

Year_____ Make_____ Model_____

Odometer_____ VIN _____

Learning Objective/Task	CDX Tasksheet Number	2008 NATEF Reference Number	2008 NATEF Priority Level
• Remove, inspect, and install stabilizer bar bushings, brackets, and links.	C793	4C9	P-2
• Remove, inspect, and install short and long arm suspension system coil springs and spring insulators.	C193	4C7	P-3
• Remove, inspect, and install steering knuckle assemblies.	C192	4C6	P-2
• Remove, inspect, and install upper and lower control arms, bushings, shafts, and rebound bumpers.	C790	4C3	P-2
• Remove, inspect, and install upper and/or lower ball joints.	C792	4C5	P-1
• Lubricate suspension and steering systems.	C616	4D6	P-2

Time off_____

Time on_____

Total time_____

Recommended Resource Materials

- CDX Automotive program
- Technical service bulletins, shop manuals, and any other information applicable to the specific vehicle or components you are working on
- Class notes

Materials Required

- Vehicle equipped with short and long arm suspension
- Spring compressor
- Torque wrench
- Manufacturer- and job-specific tools
- Grease gun with specified grease

Some Safety Issues to Consider

- Lifting equipment such as vehicle jacks and stands, and vehicle hoists are important tools that increase productivity and make the job easier. But they can also cause severe injury or death if used improperly. Make sure you follow the manufacturer's operation procedures. Also, make sure you have your supervisor/instructor's permission to use any particular type of lifting equipment.
- Some suspension systems are electronically controlled, and can raise or lower without notice. Please familiarize yourself with the manufacturer's safety precautions related to these procedures.
- Vehicle springs store a lot of energy which, if released improperly, can cause injury or death. Please familiarize yourself with the manufacturer's safety precautions related to these procedures.
- Always wear the correct protective eyewear and clothing and use the appropriate safety equipment, as well as fender covers, seat protectors, and floor mat protectors.
- Make sure you understand and observe all legislative and personal safety procedures when carrying out practical assignments. If you are unsure of what these are, ask your supervisor/instructor.

Performance Standard

0—No exposure: No information or practice provided during the program; complete training required

1—Exposure only: General information provided with no practice time; close supervision needed; additional training required

2—Limited practice: Has practiced job during training program; additional training required to develop skill

3—Moderately skilled: Has performed job independently during training program; limited additional training may be required

4—Skilled: Can perform job independently with no additional training

▶ **TASK** Remove, inspect, and install stabilizer bar bushings, brackets, and links.　　C793 4C9

1. Research the disassembly and inspection procedure for the stabilizer bar, bushings, brackets, and links in the appropriate service information.
   a. List any precautions:

   b. List, or print off and attach to this sheet, the steps to disassemble the stabilizer bar system.

2. Safely raise and support the vehicle.
3. Following the instructions and all the safety precautions outlined in the shop manual, dismantle, clean, and inspect the stabilizer bar, bushings, and links. List your observation/s:
   a. Stabilizer bar:

   b. Bushing/s:

   c. Link/s:

4. Determine any necessary action/s:

The rest of this task is completed by performing the remainder of the tasks, and can be signed off at the end of this tasksheet. Please refer to page 50 for the completion of this task.

▶ **TASK** Remove, inspect, and install short and long arm suspension system coil
springs and spring insulators.　　C193 4C7

1. Research the disassembly and inspection procedure for the coil springs and spring insulators in the appropriate service information.
   a. List any precautions:

   b. List, or print off and attach to this sheet, the steps to disassemble the coil springs.

2. Have your supervisor/instructor verify your listed precautions and procedures.
   a. Supervisor/instructor initials: _____

3. Following the instructions and all the safety precautions outlined in the shop manual, remove, clean, and inspect the coil spring and spring insulators. List your observation/s:
   a. Coil spring:

   b. Spring insulators:

4. Determine any necessary action/s:

The rest of this task is completed by performing the remainder of the tasks, and can be signed off at the end of this tasksheet. Please refer to page 50 for the completion of this task.

▶ **TASK** Remove, inspect, and install steering knuckle assemblies. | C192 4C6

Time off_____

Time on_____

Total time_____

1. Research the disassembly and inspection procedure for the steering knuckle assembly in the appropriate service information.
   a. List any precautions:

   b. List, or print off and attach to this sheet, the steps to disassemble the steering knuckle assembly.

2. Following the instructions and all the safety precautions outlined in the shop manual, remove, clean, and inspect the steering knuckle assembly. List your observation/s:
   a. Steering knuckle:

3. Determine any necessary action/s:

The rest of this task is completed by performing the remainder of the tasks, and can be signed off at the end of this tasksheet. Please refer to page 50 for the completion of this task.

▶ **TASK** Remove, inspect, and install upper and lower control arms, bushings, shafts, and rebound bumpers. | C790 4C3

Time off_____

Time on_____

Total time_____

1. Research the disassembly and inspection procedure for the upper and lower control arms, bushings, shafts, and rebound bumpers in the appropriate service information.
   a. List any precautions:

b. List, or print off and attach to this sheet, the steps to disassemble the control arms.

2. Following the instructions and all the safety precautions outlined in the shop manual, remove, clean, and inspect the upper and lower control arms, bushings, shafts, and rebound bumpers. List your observation/s:
   a. Upper control arm:

   b. Lower control arm:

   c. Bushings:

   d. Shafts:

   e. Rebound bumper/s:

3. Determine any necessary action/s:

The rest of this task is completed by performing the remainder of the tasks, and can be signed off at the end of this tasksheet. Please refer to page 51 for the completion of this task.

▶ **TASK** Remove, inspect, and install upper and/or lower ball joints. `C792 4C5`

Total time

Time on

Time off

1. Research the disassembly and inspection procedure for the upper and/or lower ball joints in the appropriate service information.
   a. List any precautions:

   b. List, or print off and attach to this sheet, the steps to disassemble the upper and/or lower ball joints.

2. Following the instructions and all the safety precautions outlined in the shop manual, remove, clean, and inspect the upper and/or lower ball joints. List your observation/s:
   a. Upper ball joint:

   b. Lower ball joint:

3. Determine any necessary action/s:

4. Have your instructor verify the removal of all suspension components and check your observations and necessary actions. Get permission to reassemble the assembly.
   a. Supervisor/instructor initials: _____

> **NOTE ▸** At this time, replace/reinstall all removed suspension components following the manufacturer's procedures and precautions. Be sure to tighten all fasteners to their specified torque and replace any retaining devices such as cotter pins and nylon locking nuts. Be careful to route all wires, hoses, and tubes in their original factory position.

5. Inspect the reassembled suspension unit for any loose fasteners, improperly installed components, etc. List your observations here:

6. Determine any necessary action/s:

7. Have your supervisor/instructor verify satisfactory completion of this procedure, any observations found, and any necessary action/s recommended.

Performance Rating

CDX Tasksheet Number: C792   **2008 NATEF Reference Number: 4C5**

☐	☐	☐	☐	☐
0	1	2	3	4

Supervisor/instructor signature _____ Date_____

▶ **TASK** Lubricate suspension and steering systems.   C616 4D6

Time off_____

1. Research the specified lubricants for lubricating the suspension grease fittings in the appropriate service information.

   Time on_____

   a. Specified grease: _____
   b. List locations of grease fittings:

   Total time_____

2. Lubricate the suspension and steering systems. Be careful not to overfill any of the joints. If done properly, grease will not be pushed out of the seals.
3. List any observation/s:

4. Have your supervisor/instructor verify satisfactory completion of this procedure, any observations found, and any necessary action/s recommended.

Performance Rating

CDX Tasksheet Number: C616   2008 NATEF Reference Number: 4D6

☐ 0   ☐ 1   ☐ 2   ☐ 3   ☐ 4

Supervisor/instructor signature _____ Date_____

▶ TASK C793/4C9 Continued Remove, inspect, and install stabilizer bar bushings, brackets, and links.

5. Have your supervisor/instructor verify satisfactory completion of this procedure, any observations found, and any necessary action/s recommended.

Performance Rating

CDX Tasksheet Number: C793   2008 NATEF Reference Number: 4C9

☐ 0   ☐ 1   ☐ 2   ☐ 3   ☐ 4

Supervisor/instructor signature _____ Date_____

▶ TASK C193/4C7 Continued Remove, inspect, and install short and long arm suspension system coil springs and spring insulators.

5. Have your supervisor/instructor verify satisfactory completion of this procedure, any observations found, and any necessary action/s recommended.

Performance Rating

CDX Tasksheet Number: C193   2008 NATEF Reference Number: 4C7

☐ 0   ☐ 1   ☐ 2   ☐ 3   ☐ 4

Supervisor/instructor signature _____ Date_____

▶ TASK C192/4C6 Continued Remove, inspect, and install steering knuckle assemblies.

4. Have your supervisor/instructor verify satisfactory completion of this procedure, any observations found, and any necessary action/s recommended.

Performance Rating

CDX Tasksheet Number: C192   2008 NATEF Reference Number: 4C6

☐ 0   ☐ 1   ☐ 2   ☐ 3   ☐ 4

Supervisor/instructor signature _____ Date_____

Time off_____

Time on_____

Total time_____

4. Have your supervisor/instructor verify satisfactory completion of this procedure, any observations found, and any necessary action/s recommended.

Performance Rating

CDX Tasksheet Number: C790   **2008 NATEF Reference Number: 4C3**

☐	☐	☐	☐	☐
0	1	2	3	4

Supervisor/instructor signature _____ Date_____

Front Suspension Service—Strut and Torsion Bar

Student/intern information:

Name_____ Date_____ Class_____

Vehicle used for this activity:

Year_____ Make_____ Model_____

Odometer_____ VIN _____

Learning Objective/Task	CDX Tasksheet Number	2008 NATEF Reference Number	2008 NATEF Priority Level
• Remove, inspect, and install strut cartridge or assembly, strut coil spring, insulators (silencers), and upper strut bearing mount.	C794	4C10	P-1
• Remove, inspect, and install strut rods and bushings.	C791	4C4	P-2
• Remove, inspect, install, and adjust suspension system torsion bars; inspect mounts.	C194	4C8	P-3

Time off_____

Time on_____

Total time_____

Recommended Resource Materials

- CDX Automotive program
- Technical service bulletins, shop manuals, and any other information applicable to the specific vehicle or components you are working on
- Class notes

Materials Required

- Vehicle equipped with strut suspension
- Vehicle with torsion bar suspension
- Strut compressor
- Torque wrench
- Manufacturer- and job-specific tools

Some Safety Issues to Consider

- Lifting equipment such as vehicle jacks and stands, and vehicle hoists are important tools that increase productivity and make the job easier. But they can also cause severe injury or death if used improperly. Make sure you follow the manufacturer's operation procedures. Also, make sure you have your supervisor/instructor's permission to use any particular type of lifting equipment.
- Some suspension systems are electronically controlled, and can raise or lower without notice. Please familiarize yourself with the manufacturer's safety precautions related to these procedures.
- Vehicle springs store a lot of energy which, if released improperly, can cause injury or death. Please familiarize yourself with the manufacturer's safety precautions related to these procedures.
- Always wear the correct protective eyewear and clothing and use the appropriate safety equipment, as well as fender covers, seat protectors, and floor mat protectors.
- Make sure you understand and observe all legislative and personal safety procedures when carrying out practical assignments. If you are unsure of what these are, ask your supervisor/instructor.

Performance Standard

0—No exposure: No information or practice provided during the program; complete training required

1—Exposure only: General information provided with no practice time; close supervision needed; additional training required

2—Limited practice: Has practiced job during training program; additional training required to develop skill

3—Moderately skilled: Has performed job independently during training program; limited additional training may be required

4—Skilled: Can perform job independently with no additional training

▶ **TASK** Remove, inspect, and install strut cartridge or assembly, strut coil spring, insulators (silencers), and upper strut bearing mount.

1. Research the disassembly and inspection procedure for the strut cartridge or assembly, strut coil spring, insulators (silencers), and upper strut bearing mount.
   a. List any precautions:

   b. List, or print off and attach to this sheet, the steps to remove and disassemble the strut assembly:

2. Have your supervisor/instructor verify your listed precautions and procedures.
   a. Supervisor/instructor initials: _____

3. Safely raise and support the vehicle.

4. Following the instructions and all the safety precautions outlined in the shop manual, remove the strut assembly from the vehicle.

NOTE ▶ On some vehicles, it makes sense to mark the position of the adjustable components so they can be reinstalled into their original positions.

5. Following the instructions and all safety precautions outlined in the shop manual, disassemble the strut. Improperly removing the spring can cause severe injury or death.

6. Clean and inspect the strut cartridge or assembly, strut coil spring, insulators (silencers), and upper strut bearing mount. List your observation/s:
   a. Strut cartridge or assembly:

   b. Strut coil spring:

   c. Spring insulators:

   d. Upper strut bearing mount:

7. Determine any necessary action/s:

NOTE ▶ You may be able to continue on with the next task **C791: Remove, inspect, and install strut rods and bushings** while you have the strut removed. If so, return to this point once you have that task completed.

8. Have your instructor verify the removal and disassembly of the strut, and check your observations and necessary actions. Get permission to reassemble the strut.
   a. Supervisor/instructor initials: _____

9. Reassemble the strut according to the manufacturer's procedure and precautions. Be careful when compressing and installing the spring as it can cause severe injury or death if installed improperly.

10. Reinstall the strut into the vehicle. Be sure to tighten all fasteners to their specified torque and replace any retaining devices such as cotter pins and nylon locking nuts. Be careful to route all wires, hoses, and tubes in their original factory positions.

11. Inspect the reassembled strut assembly for any loose fasteners, improperly installed components, etc. List your observations here:

12. Determine any necessary action/s:

13. Have your supervisor/instructor verify satisfactory completion of this procedure, any observations found, and any necessary action/s recommended.

Performance Rating

		CDX Tasksheet Number: C794	2008 NATEF Reference Number: 4C10	
☐	☐	☐	☐	☐
0	1	2	3	4

Supervisor/instructor signature _____ Date_____

▶ **TASK** Remove, inspect, and install strut rods and bushings.   C791 4C4

1. Research the disassembly and inspection procedure for the strut rods and bushings in the appropriate service information.
   a. List any precautions:

   b. List, or print off and attach to this sheet, the steps to disassemble the strut rods and bushings:

2. Following the instructions and all the safety precautions outlined in the shop manual, remove the strut rods and bushings from the vehicle. List your observation/s:
   a. Strut rod:

   b. Bushings:

3. Determine any necessary action/s:

Time off_____

Time on_____

Total time_____

4. Have your instructor verify the removal and disassembly of the strut rod and bushings, and check your observations and necessary actions. Also, have your instructor sign off on the disassembly of the strut in the previous task.
   a. Supervisor/instructor initials: _____

5. Reassemble the strut rods and bushings according to the manufacturer's procedure and precautions.

> **NOTE ▸** Return to task **C794: Remove, inspect, and install strut cartridge or assembly, strut coil spring, insulators (silencers), and upper strut bearing mount** step 6.

6. Have your supervisor/instructor verify satisfactory completion of this procedure, any observations found, and any necessary action/s recommended.

Performance Rating

		CDX Tasksheet Number: C791	**2008 NATEF Reference Number: 4C4**

☐   ☐   ☐   ☐   ☐

0   1   2   3   4

Supervisor/instructor signature _____ Date_____

Total time

Time on

Time off

▸ TASK Remove, inspect, install, and adjust suspension system torsion bars; inspect mounts.

C194   4C8

Vehicle used for this activity:

Year_____ Make_____ Model_____

Odometer_____ VIN _____

1. Research the disassembly and inspection procedure for the torsion bars and mounts in the appropriate service information.
   a. List any precautions:

   b. List, or print off and attach to this sheet, the steps to remove the torsion bar:

   c. List the flat rate time to remove and install one torsion bar: _____ hrs
   d. Specified ride height: _____

2. Have your supervisor/instructor verify your listed precautions and procedures.
   a. Supervisor/instructor initials: _____

3. Measure and record vehicle ride height. Note your findings here:

4. Safely raise and support the vehicle.

5. Following the instructions and all the safety precautions outlined in the shop manual, remove one torsion bar from the vehicle. List your observation/s:

   a. Torsion bar:

   b. Mounts:

   c. Height adjustment mechanism:

   d. Bushing/s:

6. Determine any necessary action/s:

7. Have your instructor verify the removal and disassembly of the torsion bar, and check your observations and necessary actions.

   a. Supervisor/instructor initials: _____

8. Reinstall the torsion bar according to the manufacturer's procedure and precautions. Be careful when installing and compressing the spring as it can cause severe injury or death if installed improperly.

9. Torque all retaining bolts to the manufacturer's specifications.

10. Following the manufacturer's procedure, adjust the ride height of the vehicle to meet specifications.

11. Inspect the suspension for any loose fasteners, improperly installed components, etc. List your observations here:

12. Determine any necessary action/s:

13. Have your supervisor/instructor verify satisfactory completion of this procedure, any observations found, and any necessary action/s recommended.

Performance Rating

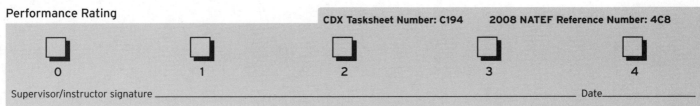

CDX Tasksheet Number: C194   2008 NATEF Reference Number: 4C8

| 0 | 1 | 2 | 3 | 4 |

Supervisor/instructor signature _____ Date_____

© Jones and Bartlett Publishers, LLC

Front Suspension Diagnosis

Student/intern information:

Name_____ Date_____ Class_____

Vehicle used for this activity:

Year_____ Make_____ Model_____

Odometer_____ VIN _____

Learning Objective/Task	CDX Tasksheet Number	2008 NATEF Reference Number	2008 NATEF Priority Level
• Diagnose short and long arm suspension system noises, body sway, and uneven ride height concerns; determine necessary action.	C852	4C1	P-1
• Diagnose strut suspension system noises, body sway, and uneven ride height concerns; determine necessary action.	C853	4C2	P-1

Time off_____

Time on_____

Total time_____

Recommended Resource Materials

- CDX Automotive program
- Technical service bulletins, shop manuals, and any other information applicable to the specific vehicle or components you are working on
- Class notes

Materials Required

- Vehicle hoist
- Vehicle with short and long arm suspension system concern
- Vehicle with strut suspension system concern
- Depending on the type of concern, special diagnostic tools may be required. See your supervisor/instructor for instructions to identify what tools may be required.

Some Safety Issues to Consider

- When running any vehicles in the shop, make sure you use the shop's exhaust ventilation system to discharge all exhaust gas safely outside.
- Lifting equipment such as vehicle jacks and stands, vehicle hoists, and engine hoists are important tools that increase productivity and make the job easier. But they can also cause severe injury or death if used improperly. Make sure you follow the manufacturer's operation procedures. Also, make sure you have your supervisor/instructor's permission to use any particular type of lifting equipment.
- Vehicle springs store a lot of energy which, if released improperly, can cause injury or death. Please familiarize yourself with the manufacturer's safety precautions related to these procedures.
- Some suspension systems are electronically controlled and can raise or lower without notice. Please familiarize yourself with the manufacturer's safety precautions related to these procedures.
- Always wear the correct protective eyewear and clothing and use the appropriate safety equipment, as well as fender covers, seat protectors, and floor mat protectors.
- Make sure you understand and observe all legislative and personal safety procedures when carrying out practical assignments. If you are unsure of what these are, ask your supervisor/instructor.

Performance Standard

0—No exposure: No information or practice provided during the program; complete training required

1—Exposure only: General information provided with no practice time; close supervision needed; additional training required

2—Limited practice: Has practiced job during training program; additional training required to develop skill

3—Moderately skilled: Has performed job independently during training program; limited additional training may be required

4—Skilled: Can perform job independently with no additional training

▶ **TASK** Diagnose short and long arm suspension system noises, body sway, and uneven ride height concerns; determine necessary action.

C852 4C1

1. List the short and long arm suspension system-related customer concern:

2. Verify the concern and list your observations here:

3. Research the possible causes for this concern in the appropriate service manual.
   a. List, or print off and attach to this sheet, the possible causes:

   b. List, or print off and attach to this sheet, the procedure for diagnosing the concern:

4. Follow the service manual procedure to diagnose the concern. List your tests and results here:

5. List the cause of the concern:

6. Determine any necessary action/s to correct the fault:

7. Have your supervisor/instructor verify satisfactory completion of this procedure, any observations found, and any necessary action/s recommended.

Performance Rating

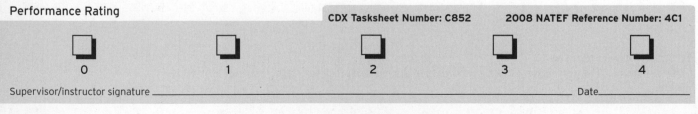

CDX Tasksheet Number: C852   2008 NATEF Reference Number: 4C1

| 0 | 1 | 2 | 3 | 4 |

Supervisor/instructor signature _____ Date_____

© Jones and Bartlett Publishers, LLC

Diagnose strut suspension system noises, body sway, and uneven ride
height concerns; determine necessary action.

C853 4C2

Time off_____

Time on_____

Total time_____

Vehicle used for this activity:

Year_____ Make_____ Model_____

Odometer_____ VIN _____

1. List the strut suspension system-related customer concern:

2. Verify the concern and list your observations here:

3. Research the possible causes for this concern in the appropriate service manual.
   a. List, or print off and attach to this sheet, the possible causes:

   b. List, or print off and attach to this sheet, the procedure for diagnosing the concern:

4. Follow the service manual procedure to diagnose the concern. List your tests and results here:

5. List the cause of the concern:

6. Determine any necessary action/s to correct the fault:

7. Have your supervisor/instructor verify satisfactory completion of this procedure, any observations found,
   and any necessary action/s recommended.

Performance Rating

CDX Tasksheet Number: C853   2008 NATEF Reference Number: 4C2

☐	☐	☐	☐	☐
0	1	2	3	4

Supervisor/instructor signature _____ Date_____

Rear Suspension Service

Student/intern information:

Name_____ Date_____ Class_____

Vehicle used for this activity:

Year_____ Make_____ Model_____

Odometer_____ VIN _____

© Jones and Bartlett Publishers, LLC

Learning Objective/Task	CDX Tasksheet Number	2008 NATEF Reference Number	2008 NATEF Priority Level
• Inspect, remove, and replace shock absorbers.	C202	4D1	P-1
• Remove, inspect, and install leaf springs, leaf spring insulators (silencers), shackles, brackets, bushings, and mounts.	C854	4C11	P-3
• Remove, inspect, and service or replace front and rear wheel bearings.	C203	4D2	P-1

Time off_____

Time on_____

Total time_____

Recommended Resource Materials

- CDX Automotive program
- Technical service bulletins, shop manuals, and any other information applicable to the specific vehicle or components you are working on
- Class notes

Materials Required

- Vehicle with hydraulic shock absorbers and leaf springs
- Vehicle lifting equipment
- Safety stands
- Manufacturer- and job-specific tools
- Specified wheel bearing grease
- New cotter pin/s, depending on application

Some Safety Issues to Consider

- Vehicle hoists are important tools that increase productivity and make the job easier. But they also can cause severe injury or death if used improperly. Make sure you follow the hoist and vehicle manufacturer's operation procedures. Also make sure you have your supervisor/instructor's permission to use a vehicle hoist.
- Shock absorbers may be the primary fastening device for holding the suspension, or axle assembly, in the vehicle. Be sure to support the suspension with the appropriate safety stands.
- Some shock absorbers are pressurized with nitrogen gas. Keep your fingers from being pinched by an expanding shock absorber.
- Some shock absorbers have overload springs attached to them. Be careful not to accidentally release the spring. Serious pinching could occur.
- Some shock absorbers are electronically controlled, and can extend or retract without notice. Please familiarize yourself with the manufacturer's safety precautions related to these procedures.
- Always wear the correct protective eyewear and clothing and use the appropriate safety equipment, as well as fender covers, seat protectors, and floor mat protectors.
- Make sure you understand and observe all legislative and personal safety procedures when carrying out practical assignments. If you are unsure of what these are, ask your supervisor/instructor.

Performance Standard

0–No exposure: No information or practice provided during the program; complete training required

1–Exposure only: General information provided with no practice time; close supervision needed; additional training required

2–Limited practice: Has practiced job during training program; additional training required to develop skill

3–Moderately skilled: Has performed job independently during training program; limited additional training may be required

4–Skilled: Can perform job independently with no additional training

▶ **TASK** Inspect, remove, and replace shock absorbers. C202 4D1

1. Research the shock absorber removal and installation procedure in the appropriate service manual. Follow all directions.
   a. Shock absorber fastener torque: _____ ft-lbs/Nm
   b. List the flat rate time for this job: _____ hrs

2. Safely raise the vehicle on a hoist. Check to see that the vehicle is secure on the hoist, and then remove the shock absorbers following the service manual procedures.

> **NOTE ▶** Be sure to support the suspension, or axle assembly, with safety stands before removing the shocks.

3. Inspect the shock absorbers, rubber bushings (bushes), and mounts and list your observations:
   a. Shock absorbers:

   b. Rubber bushings (bushes):

   c. Shock mounts:

4. Determine any necessary action/s:

5. Have your supervisor/instructor verify the removal of the shock absorbers and your observations, and initial here:
   a. Supervisor/instructor's initials: _____

6. Reinstall the shock absorbers according to the service manual procedure. Be sure to torque all fasteners properly.

7. Have your supervisor/instructor verify satisfactory completion of this procedure, any observations found, and any necessary action/s recommended.

Performance Rating

		CDX Tasksheet Number: C202	**2008 NATEF Reference Number: 4D1**	
☐	☐	☐	☐	☐
0	1	2	3	4

Supervisor/instructor signature _____ Date_____

▶ **TASK** Remove, inspect, and install leaf springs, leaf spring insulators (silencers), shackles, brackets, bushings, and mounts. C854 4C11

Vehicle used for this activity:

Year_____ Make_____ Model_____

Odometer_____ VIN _____

1. Research the leaf spring removal and installation procedure in the appropriate service manual. Follow all directions.
   a. U-bolt torque: _____ ft-lbs/Nm
   b. Shackle bolt torque: _____ ft-lbs/Nm
   c. List the flat rate time for this job: _____ hrs

2. Safely raise the vehicle. Support the axle assembly with safety stands.

3. Following the instructions and all the safety precautions outlined in the shop manual, remove the leaf spring/s packs and insulators. Place components on the work bench for evaluation.

4. With reference to the appropriate shop manual section, inspect and record the condition of each of the following:

   a. Rear shackle bushings: _____

   b. Front shackle bushings: _____

   c. Spring leaf insulators: _____

   d. U-bolts and nuts: _____

   e. Rubber bump stops: _____

   f. Spring shackles and plates: _____

   g. Leaf spring pack: _____

5. Following the instructions and all the safety precautions outlined in the shop manual, remove leaf spring insulators (silencers).

6. Have your supervisor/instructor verify the removal of the leaf spring insulators (silencers) and your observations, and initial here:

   a. Supervisor/instructor's initials: _____

7. Following the instructions and all the safety precautions outlined in the shop manual, reinstall leaf spring suspension components.

8. Torque all retaining bolts to the manufacturer's specifications (if applicable).

   a. Record the torque settings used: _____

9. Return the vehicle to its beginning condition and clean and return any tools that you may have used to their proper locations.

10. Have your supervisor/instructor verify satisfactory completion of this procedure, any observations found, and any necessary action/s recommended.

Performance Rating

CDX Tasksheet Number: C854   2008 NATEF Reference Number: 4C11

☐	☐	☐	☐	☐
0	1	2	3	4

Supervisor/instructor signature _____ Date_____

▶ TASK Remove, inspect, and service or replace front and rear wheel bearings.   C203 4D2

Time off_____

Time on_____

Vehicle used for this activity:

Year_____ Make_____ Model_____

Odometer_____ VIN _____

Total time_____

1. Which wheel bearing are you servicing? _____

2. Research the wheel bearing removal, service, and installation procedure in the appropriate service manual. Follow all directions.

   a. List the bearing adjustment procedure:

   b. Specified wheel bearing grease: _____

   c. Lug nut torque: _____ ft-lbs/Nm

   d. List the flat rate time for this job: _____ hrs

3. Safely raise and support the vehicle.

4. Following the instructions and all the safety precautions outlined in the shop manual, dismantle, clean, and inspect wheel bearing and race. List your observation/s:
   a. Wheel bearing: _____
   b. Race: _____
   c. Spindle: _____
   d. Hub: _____
   e. Are these parts serviceable? **Yes/No** (Circle one)

5. Determine any necessary action/s:

6. Have your supervisor/instructor verify the removal of the wheel bearings and your observations, and initial here:
   a. Supervisor/instructor's initials: _____

7. Repack (if applicable) the wheel bearings with the specified grease.

8. Following the instructions and all the safety precautions outlined in the shop manual, reinstall and adjust the wheel bearing assembly. Before locking the adjustment nut, have your supervisor/instructor verify the wheel bearing adjustment.
   a. Supervisor/instructor's initials: _____

9. Following the manufacturer's procedure, lock the wheel bearing adjustment nut with the specified retaining device. Always replace disposable devices such as cotter pins with new parts.

10. Return the vehicle to its beginning condition and clean and return any tools that you may have used to their proper locations.

11. Have your supervisor/instructor verify satisfactory completion of this procedure, any observations found, and any necessary action/s recommended.

Performance Rating

		CDX Tasksheet Number: C203	2008 NATEF Reference Number: 4D2	
☐	☐	☐	☐	☐
0	1	2	3	4

Supervisor/instructor signature _____ Date_____

Electronically Controlled Steering and Suspension Service

Student/intern information:

Name_____ Date_____ Class_____

Vehicle used for this activity:

Year_____ Make_____ Model_____

Odometer_____ VIN _____

Learning Objective/Task	CDX Tasksheet Number	2008 NATEF Reference Number	2008 NATEF Priority Level
• Inspect and test electric power assist steering.	C700	4B20	P-3
• Test and diagnose components of electronically controlled steering systems using a scan tool; determine necessary action.	C186	4B19	P-3
• Diagnose, inspect, adjust, repair, or replace components of electronically controlled steering systems (including sensors, switches, and actuators); initialize system as required.	C614	4D4	P-3
• Describe the function of the idle speed compensation switch.	C615	4D5	P-3
• Identify hybrid vehicle power steering system electrical circuits, service and safety precautions.	C551	4B21	P-3
• Test and diagnose components of electronically controlled suspension systems using a scan tool; determine necessary action.	C204	4D3	P-3

Time off_____

Time on_____

Total time_____

Recommended Resource Materials

- CDX Automotive program
- Technical service bulletins, shop manuals, and any other information applicable to the specific vehicle or components you are working on
- Class notes

Materials Required

- Vehicle with electronically controlled suspension and steering
- Scan tool
- DMM/DVOM
- Manufacturer- and job-specific tools

Some Safety Issues to Consider

- Diagnosis of this fault may require test driving the vehicle on the school grounds. Attempt this task only with full permission from your instructor and follow all guidelines and policies exactly.
- Lifting equipment such as vehicle jacks and stands, and vehicle hoists are important tools that increase productivity and make the job easier. But they can also cause severe injury or death if used improperly. Make sure you follow the manufacturer's operation procedures. Also, make sure you have your supervisor/instructor's permission to use any particular type of lifting equipment.
- Vehicle springs store a lot of energy which if released improperly, can cause injury or death. Please familiarize yourself with the manufacturer's safety precautions related to these procedures.
- Some suspension systems are electronically controlled, and can raise or lower without notice. Please familiarize yourself with the manufacturer's safety precautions related to these procedures.
- Always wear the correct protective eyewear and clothing and use the appropriate safety equipment, as well as fender covers, seat protectors, and floor mat protectors.
- Make sure you understand and observe all legislative and personal safety procedures when carrying out practical assignments. If you are unsure of what these are, ask your supervisor/instructor.

Performance Standard

0–No exposure: No information or practice provided during the program; complete training required

1–Exposure only: General information provided with no practice time; close supervision needed; additional training required

2–Limited practice: Has practiced job during training program; additional training required to develop skill

3–Moderately skilled: Has performed job independently during training program; limited additional training may be required

4–Skilled: Can perform job independently with no additional training

▶ **TASK** Inspect and test electric power assist steering. `C700  4B20`

1. Research the electric power assist steering system in the appropriate service information for the vehicle you are working on.
   a. Read the "description and operation" section.
   b. Read the "testing and diagnosis" section.
   c. List any precautions mentioned:

2. Following the service information procedure, inspect and test the electronic power steering system. List your observation/s:

3. Determine any necessary action/s:

4. Have your supervisor/instructor verify satisfactory completion of this procedure, any observations found, and any necessary action/s recommended.

Performance Rating

CDX Tasksheet Number: C700   2008 NATEF Reference Number: 4B20

☐	☐	☐	☐	☐
0	1	2	3	4

Supervisor/instructor signature _____ Date_____

▶ **TASK** Test and diagnose components of electronically controlled steering systems using a scan tool; determine necessary action. `C186  4B19`

Vehicle used for this activity:

Year_____ Make_____ Model_____

Odometer_____ VIN _____

1. List the electronically controlled steering system-related customer concern:

2. Verify the concern and list your observations here:

3. Retrieve any DTCs with a scan tool and list those DTCs here:

4. Research the possible causes for this concern in the appropriate service manual.
   a. List, or print off and attach to this sheet, the possible causes:

   b. List, or print off and attach to this sheet, the procedure for diagnosing the concern:

5. Follow the service manual procedure to diagnose the concern. List your tests and results here:

6. List the cause of the concern:

7. Determine any necessary action/s to correct the fault:

8. Have your supervisor/instructor verify satisfactory completion of this procedure, any observations found, and any necessary action/s recommended.

Performance Rating

CDX Tasksheet Number: C186   2008 NATEF Reference Number: 4B19

☐	☐	☐	☐	☐
0	1	2	3	4

Supervisor/instructor signature _____ Date_____

© Jones and Bartlett Publishers, LLC

NOTE ▶ Ask your instructor if you can continue this repair on task **C614: Diagnose, inspect, adjust, repair, or replace components of electronically controlled steering systems (including sensors, switches, and actuators); initialize system as required**. If so, skip down to step 9 and continue working.

▶ **TASK** Diagnose, inspect, adjust, repair, or replace components of electronically controlled steering systems (including sensors, switches, and actuators); initialize system as required.

C614 4D4

Vehicle used for this activity:

Year_____ Make_____ Model_____

Odometer_____ VIN _____

1. List the electronically controlled steering system-related customer concern:

2. Verify the concern and list your observations here:

3. Retrieve any DTCs with a scan tool and list those DTCs here:

4. Research the possible causes for this concern in the appropriate service manual.
   a. List, or print off and attach to this sheet, the possible causes:

   b. List, or print off and attach to this sheet, the procedure for diagnosing the concern:

   c. List, or print off and attach to this sheet, the procedure for initializing the system once repairs are completed:

5. Follow the service manual procedure to diagnose the concern. List your tests and results here:

6. List the cause of the concern:

7. Determine any necessary action/s to correct the fault:

8. Have your supervisor/instructor verify your diagnosis and get permission to make the repair.
   a. Supervisor/instructor initials: _____

9. Following the service information procedures, perform any necessary repair/s, and reinitialize the system.

10. Retest the electronically controlled power steering system operation. List your observation/s:

11. Have your supervisor/instructor verify satisfactory completion of this procedure, any observations found, and any necessary action/s recommended.

Performance Rating

CDX Tasksheet Number: C614   **2008 NATEF Reference Number: 4D4**

☐ 0   ☐ 1   ☐ 2   ☐ 3   ☐ 4

Supervisor/instructor signature _____ Date_____

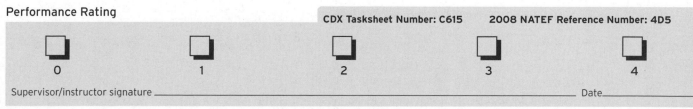

▶ **TASK** Describe the function of the idle speed compensation switch. _____ **C615 4D5**

Vehicle used for this activity:

Year_____ Make_____ Model_____

Odometer_____ VIN _____

Time off_____

Time on_____

Total time_____

1. Research the function of the idle speed compensation switch in the appropriate service manual.
   a. Describe, in your own words, the function of the idle speed compensation switch:

2. Have your supervisor/instructor verify satisfactory completion of this procedure, any observations found, and any necessary action/s recommended.

Performance Rating

CDX Tasksheet Number: C615   **2008 NATEF Reference Number: 4D5**

☐ 0   ☐ 1   ☐ 2   ☐ 3   ☐ 4

Supervisor/instructor signature _____ Date_____

▶ **TASK** Identify hybrid vehicle power steering system electrical circuits, service and safety precautions.

C551 4B21

Vehicle used for this activity:

Year_____ Make_____ Model_____

Odometer_____ VIN _____

1. Research the location and safety precautions for the power steering system the vehicle is equipped with.
   a. List the voltage that the power steering system operates at: _____ V
   b. List any safety precautions when working on or around the systems and circuits:

2. On the vehicle, locate and point out the power steering electrical circuits and components to your instructor.

3. Have your supervisor/instructor verify satisfactory completion of this procedure, any observations found, and any necessary action/s recommended.

Performance Rating

CDX Tasksheet Number: C551   2008 NATEF Reference Number: 4B21

☐   ☐   ☐   ☐   ☐
0   1   2   3   4

Supervisor/instructor signature _____ Date_____

▶ **TASK** Test and diagnose components of electronically controlled suspension systems using a scan tool; determine necessary action.

C204 4D3

Vehicle used for this activity:

Year_____ Make_____ Model_____

Odometer_____ VIN _____

1. List the electronically controlled suspension system-related customer concern:

2. Verify the concern and list your observations here:

3. Retrieve any DTCs with a scan tool and list those DTCs here:

4. Research the possible causes for this concern in the appropriate service manual.
    a. List, or print off and attach to this sheet, the possible causes:

    b. List, or print off and attach to this sheet, the procedure for diagnosing the concern:

5. Follow the service manual procedure to diagnose the concern. List your tests and results here:

6. List the cause of the concern:

7. Determine any necessary action/s to correct the fault:

8. Have your supervisor/instructor verify satisfactory completion of this procedure, any observations found, and any necessary action/s recommended.

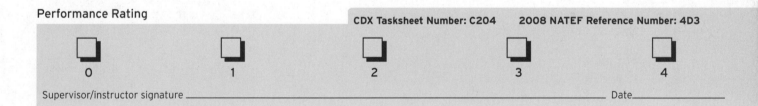

Performance Rating

CDX Tasksheet Number: C204   2008 NATEF Reference Number: 4D3

0   1   2   3   4

Supervisor/instructor signature _____ Date_____

Wheel Alignment Diagnosis, Adjustment, and Repair

Student/intern information:

Name_____ Date_____ Class_____

Vehicle used for this activity:

Year_____ Make_____ Model_____

Odometer_____ VIN _____

© Jones and Bartlett Publishers, LLC

Learning Objective/Task	CDX Tasksheet Number	2008 NATEF Reference Number	2008 NATEF Priority Level
• Diagnose vehicle wander, drift, pull, hard steering, bump steer, memory steer, torque steer, and steering return concerns; determine necessary action.	C206	4E1	P-1
• Perform prealignment inspection and measure vehicle ride height; perform necessary action.	C617	4E2	P-1
• Prepare vehicle for wheel alignment on the alignment machine; perform four wheel alignment by checking and adjusting front and rear wheel caster, camber, and toe as required; center steering wheel.	C618	4E3	P-1
• Check toe-out-on-turns (turning radius); determine necessary action.	C213	4E4	P-2
• Check SAI (steering axis inclination) and included angle; determine necessary action.	C214	4E5	P-2
• Check rear wheel thrust angle; determine necessary action.	C216	4E6	P-1
• Check for front wheel setback; determine necessary action.	C217	4E7	P-2
• Check front and/or rear cradle (subframe) alignment; determine necessary action.	C795	4E8	P-3

Time off_____

Time on_____

Total time_____

Recommended Resource Materials

- CDX Automotive program
- Technical service bulletins, shop manuals, and any other information applicable to the specific vehicle or components you are working on
- Class notes

Materials Required

- Vehicle with alignment concern
- Tire pressure gauge and inflator
- Wheel alignment machine
- Manufacturer- or job-specific tools

Some Safety Issues to Consider

- Diagnosis of this fault may require test driving the vehicle on the school grounds. Attempt this task only with full permission from your instructor and follow all guidelines and policies exactly.
- Lifting equipment such as vehicle jacks and stands, and vehicle hoists are important tools that increase productivity and make the job easier. But they can also cause severe injury or death if used improperly. Make sure you follow the manufacturer's operation procedures. Also, make sure you have your supervisor/instructor's permission to use any particular type of lifting equipment.
- Vehicle springs store a lot of energy which if released improperly, can cause injury or death. Please familiarize yourself with the manufacturer's safety precautions related to these procedures.
- Some suspension systems are electronically controlled, and can raise or lower without notice. Please familiarize yourself with the manufacturer's safety precautions related to these procedures.
- Always wear the correct protective eyewear and clothing and use the appropriate safety equipment, as well as fender covers, seat protectors, and floor mat protectors.
- Make sure you understand and observe all legislative and personal safety procedures when carrying out practical assignments. If you are unsure of what these are, ask your supervisor/instructor.

Performance Standard

0–No exposure: No information or practice provided during the program; complete training required

1–Exposure only: General information provided with no practice time; close supervision needed; additional training required

2–Limited practice: Has practiced job during training program; additional training required to develop skill

3–Moderately skilled: Has performed job independently during training program; limited additional training may be required

4–Skilled: Can perform job independently with no additional training

▶ **TASK** Diagnose vehicle wander, drift, pull, hard steering, bump steer, memory steer, torque steer, and steering return concerns; determine necessary action.

C206 4E1

Total time

Time on

Time off

1. List the wheel alignment-related customer concern:

2. Verify the concern and list your observations here:

3. Research the possible causes for this concern in the appropriate service manual.
   a. List, or print off and attach to this sheet, the possible causes:

   b. List, or print off and attach to this sheet, the procedure for diagnosing the concern:

The rest of this task is completed by performing the remainder of the tasks, and can be signed off at the end of this tasksheet. Please refer to page 81 for the completion of this task.

▶ **TASK** Perform prealignment inspection and measure vehicle ride height; perform necessary action.

C617 4E2

Total time

Time on

Time off

1. Research the prealignment process for this vehicle in the appropriate service information.
   a. List the ride height specifications:

   b. Can the right height be manually adjusted on this vehicle? **Yes/No** (Circle one)
      i.   If yes, what is the specified adjustment procedure?

   c. List the specified tire size:

   d. List the specified tire pressure/s:

   e. List any other manufacturer-specified checks:

2. Following the manufacturer's procedure, inspect the vehicle.
   a. Is the vehicle abnormally loaded? **Yes/No** (Circle one)
   b. Are the specified tires installed on the vehicle? **Yes/No** (Circle one)
   c. List the condition and wear of each tire as you inflate the tires to proper pressure:
      i.   Left front: _____
      ii. Right front: _____
      iii. Right rear: _____
      iv. Left rear: _____
   d. Does the vehicle meet the specified ride height? **Yes/No** (Circle one)
   e. List the results of other specified checks:

3. Determine any necessary action/s:

4. Does the vehicle meet the prealignment inspection requirements for an alignment? **Yes/No** (Circle one)
5. Have your supervisor/instructor verify satisfactory completion of this procedure, any observations found, and any necessary action/s recommended.

Performance Rating

CDX Tasksheet Number: C617   2008 NATEF Reference Number: 4E2

☐	☐	☐	☐	☐
0	1	2	3	4

Supervisor/instructor signature _____ Date_____

▶ **TASK** Prepare vehicle for wheel alignment on the alignment machine; perform four wheel alignment by checking and adjusting front and rear wheel caster, camber, and toe as required; center steering wheel.   **C618 4E3**

Time off_____

Time on_____

1. Prepare the vehicle for wheel alignment on the alignment machine.
2. Perform four wheel alignment measurements and list the following readings:

   Front wheel:
   a. Caster: LF: _____ RF: _____ Specs: _____
   b. Cross caster: Measured: _____ Specs: _____
   c. Camber: LF: _____ RF: _____ Specs: _____
   d. Cross camber: Measured: _____ Specs: _____
   e. Toe: LF: _____ RF: _____ Specs: _____
   f. Total toe: Measured: _____ Specs: _____

   Rear wheel:
   g. Caster: LF: _____ RF: _____ Specs: _____
   h. Cross caster: Measured: _____ Specs: _____
   i. Camber: LF: _____ RF: _____ Specs: _____
   j. Cross camber: Measured: _____ Specs: _____
   k. Toe: LF: _____ RF: _____ Specs: _____
   l. Total toe: Measured: _____ Specs: _____

Total time_____

3. Determine any necessary action/s:

It will be more efficient if you perform the remainder of the measurement tasks before making any further adjustments to the caster, camber, and toe as those measurements may identify additional service or repair needs. The rest of this task is completed by performing the remainder of the tasks, and can be signed off at the end of this tasksheet. Please refer to page 80 for the completion of this task.

▶ **TASK** Check toe-out-on-turns (turning radius); determine necessary action.   C213 4E4

1. Following the manufacturer's procedure, measure toe-out-on-turns.
   a. LF wheel set at: _____ degrees
   b. RF wheel measures: _____ degrees
   c. RF wheel set at: _____ degrees
   d. LF wheel measures: _____ degrees
2. Determine any necessary action/s:

The rest of this task is completed by performing the remainder of the tasks, and can be signed off at the end of this tasksheet. Please refer to page 81 for the completion of this task.

▶ **TASK** Check SAI (steering axis inclination) and included angle; determine
necessary action.   C214 4E5

1. Following the manufacturer's procedure, measure SAI (steering axis inclination) and included angle.
   a. Manufacturer's specifications:

   b. Measured angles:

2. Determine any necessary action/s:

The rest of this task is completed by performing the remainder of the tasks, and can be signed off at the end of this tasksheet. Please refer to page 81 for the completion of this task.

▶ **TASK** Check rear wheel thrust angle; determine necessary action.   C216 4E6

1. Following the manufacturer's procedure, measure the rear wheel thrust angle.
   a. Manufacturer's specifications:

   b. Measured thrust angle:

2. Determine any necessary action/s:

The rest of this task is completed by performing the remainder of the tasks, and can be signed off at the end of this tasksheet. Please refer to page 81 for the completion of this task.

▶ **TASK** Check for front wheel setback; determine necessary action.   C217   4E7

Time off_____

Time on_____

Total time_____

1. Following the manufacturer's procedure, check for front wheel setback.
    a. Manufacturer's specifications:

    b. Measured setback:

2. Determine any necessary action/s:

3. Have your supervisor/instructor verify all of your measurements and necessary actions for all of the previous tasks. Get permission to perform the necessary action/s.
    a. Supervisor/instructor initials: _____

4. Perform all of the adjustments necessary for a four wheel alignment as listed in the previous tasks.

5. When finished, re-measure all alignment angles to make sure they are within specifications.

6. List, or print off and attach to this sheet, the post-alignment measurements.

    Front wheel:
    a. Caster: LF: _____ RF: _____ Specs: _____
    b. Cross caster: Measured: _____ Specs: _____
    c. Camber: LF: _____ RF: _____ Specs: _____
    d. Cross camber: Measured: _____ Specs: _____
    e. Toe: LF: _____ RF: _____ Specs: _____
    f. Total toe: Measured: _____ Specs: _____

    Rear wheel:
    g. Caster: LF: _____ RF: _____ Specs: _____
    h. Cross caster: Measured: _____ Specs: _____
    i. Camber: LF: _____ RF: _____ Specs: _____
    j. Cross camber: Measured: _____ Specs: _____
    k. Toe: LF: _____ RF: _____ Specs: _____
    l. Total toe: Measured: _____ Specs: _____

    Toe-out-on-turns:
    m. LF wheel set at: _____ degrees
    n. RF wheel measures: _____ degrees
    o. RF wheel set at: _____ degrees
    p. LF wheel measures: _____ degrees

7. List the measurement/s for SAI and included angle:

8. List the measurement/s for rear wheel thrust angle:

9. List the measurement/s for front wheel setback:

10. Do all the angles meet the manufacturer's specifications? **Yes/No** (Circle one)
11. Determine any further necessary action/s:

12. Inspect the vehicle for any loose or missing fasteners or improper repairs. List your observation/s:

13. Have your supervisor/instructor verify satisfactory completion of this procedure, any observations found, and any necessary action/s recommended.

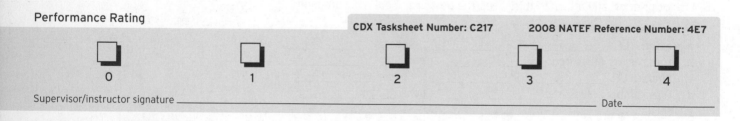

Performance Rating

CDX Tasksheet Number: C217   2008 NATEF Reference Number: 4E7

0   1   2   3   4

Supervisor/instructor signature _____ Date_____

Total time

▶ **TASK** C618/4E3 Continued Prepare vehicle for wheel alignment on the alignment machine; perform four wheel alignment by checking and adjusting front and rear wheel caster, camber, and toe as required; center steering wheel.

4. Have your supervisor/instructor verify satisfactory completion of this procedure, any observations found, and any necessary action/s recommended.

Time on

Time off

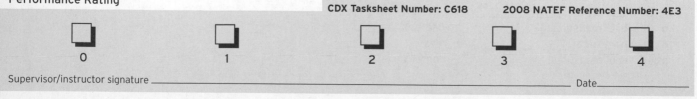

Performance Rating

CDX Tasksheet Number: C618   2008 NATEF Reference Number: 4E3

0   1   2   3   4

Supervisor/instructor signature _____ Date_____

► **TASK** **C213/4E4 Continued** Check toe-out-on-turns (turning radius); determine necessary action.

3. Have your supervisor/instructor verify satisfactory completion of this procedure, any observations found, and any necessary action/s recommended.

Performance Rating

CDX Tasksheet Number: C213   2008 NATEF Reference Number: 4E4

☐   ☐   ☐   ☐   ☐
0   1   2   3   4

Supervisor/instructor signature _____ Date_____

► **TASK** **C214/4E5 Continued** Check SAI (steering axis inclination) and included angle; determine necessary action.

3. Have your supervisor/instructor verify satisfactory completion of this procedure, any observations found, and any necessary action/s recommended.

Performance Rating

CDX Tasksheet Number: C214   2008 NATEF Reference Number: 4E5

☐   ☐   ☐   ☐   ☐
0   1   2   3   4

Supervisor/instructor signature _____ Date_____

► **TASK** **C216/4E6 Continued** Check rear wheel thrust angle; determine necessary action.

3. Have your supervisor/instructor verify satisfactory completion of this procedure, any observations found, and any necessary action/s recommended.

Performance Rating

CDX Tasksheet Number: C216   2008 NATEF Reference Number: 4E6

☐   ☐   ☐   ☐   ☐
0   1   2   3   4

Supervisor/instructor signature _____ Date_____

► **TASK** **C206/4E1 Continued** Diagnose vehicle wander, drift, pull, hard steering, bump steer, memory steer, torque steer, and steering return concerns; determine necessary action.

4. Reflecting back over these tasks, complete the 3Cs which you started above.
   a. List the customer concern/s:

b. List the cause/s of the concern/s:

c. List the action/s necessary to correct the fault/s:

5. Have your supervisor/instructor verify satisfactory completion of this procedure, any observations found, and any necessary action/s recommended.

Performance Rating

☐   ☐   ☐   ☐   ☐
0   1   2   3   4

Supervisor/instructor signature _____ Date_____

Total time

Time on

Time off

▶ **TASK** Check front and/or rear cradle (subframe) alignment; determine necessary action.   C795 4E8

Vehicle used for this activity:

Year_____ Make_____ Model_____

Odometer_____ VIN _____

1. Following the manufacturer's procedure, check front and rear cradle alignment.
   a. Manufacturer's specifications:

   b. Measured cradle alignment:

2. Determine any necessary action/s:

3. Have your supervisor/instructor verify satisfactory completion of this procedure, any observations found, and any necessary action/s recommended.

Performance Rating

☐   ☐   ☐   ☐   ☐
0   1   2   3   4

Supervisor/instructor signature _____ Date_____

Appendix A: CDX/NATEF Correlation Guide for ASE 4: Suspension and Steering

A. General Suspension and Steering Systems Diagnosis

NATEF 2008 Reference and Priority	NATEF 2005 Reference and Priority	Tasksheet Title	2008 CDX Tasksheet Number	2005 CDX Tasksheet Number	Page(s)
4A1; P-1	4A01; P-1	Complete work order to include customer information, vehicle identifying information, customer concern, related service history, cause, and correction.	C879	C549	1-2, 4
4A2; P-1	4A02; P-1	Identify and interpret suspension and steering system concerns; determine necessary action.	C851	C165	1, 3-4
4A3; P-1	4A03; P-1	Research applicable vehicle and service information, such as suspension and steering system operation, vehicle service history, service precautions, and technical service bulletins.	C166	C166	1-3
4A4; P-1	4A04; P-1	Locate and interpret vehicle and major component identification numbers.	C872	C167	1-2

B. Steering Systems Diagnosis and Repair

NATEF 2008 Reference and Priority	NATEF 2005 Reference and Priority	Tasksheet Title	2008 CDX Tasksheet Number	2005 CDX Tasksheet Number	Page(s)
4B1; P-1	4B01; P-1	Disable and enable supplemental restraint system (SRS).	C168	C168	39-40
4B2; P-1	4B02; P-1	Remove and replace steering wheel; center/time supplemental restraint system (SRS) coil (clock spring).	C169	C169	39-41
4B3; P-2	4B03; P-2	Diagnose steering column noises, looseness, and binding concerns (including tilt mechanisms); determine necessary action.	C170	C170	39, 42-43
4B4; P-2	4B04; P-3	Diagnose power steering gear (non-rack and pinion) binding, uneven turning effort, looseness, hard steering, and noise concerns; determine necessary action.	C884	C171	35-36
4B5; P-2	4B05; P-3	Diagnose power steering gear (rack and pinion) binding, uneven turning effort, looseness, hard steering, and noise concerns; determine necessary action.	C880	C172	35, 37
4B6; P-2	4B06; P-2	Inspect steering shaft universal-joint(s), flexible coupling(s), collapsible column, lock cylinder mechanism, and steering wheel; perform necessary action.	C173	C173	39, 41-42
4B7; P-3	4B07; P-3	Adjust non-rack and pinion worm bearing preload and sector lash.	C881	C174	31, 33-34
4B8; P-2	4B08; P-1	Remove and replace rack and pinion steering gear; inspect mounting bushings and brackets.	C882	C175	31-32

NATEF 2008 Reference and Priority	NATEF 2005 Reference and Priority	Tasksheet Title	2008 CDX Tasksheet Number	2005 CDX Tasksheet Number	Page(s)
4B9; P-2	4B09; P-1	Inspect and replace rack and pinion steering gear inner tie rod ends (sockets) and bellows boots.	C883	C176	31, 33
4B10; P-1	4B10; P-1	Determine proper power steering fluid type; inspect fluid level and condition.	C177	C177	19-20
4B11; P-2	4B11; P-2	Flush, fill, and bleed power steering system.	C178	C178	19, 21
4B12; P-2	4B12; P-2	Diagnose power steering fluid leakage; determine necessary action.	C179	C179	19, 25
4B13; P-1	4B13; P-1	Remove, inspect, replace, and adjust power steering pump belt.	C180	C180	19, 21-22
4B14; P-2	4B14; P-3	Remove and reinstall power steering pump.	C181	C181	19, 22-23
4B15; P-2	4B15; P-3	Remove and reinstall press fit power steering pump pulley; check pulley and belt alignment.	C699	C182	19, 23-24
4B16; P-2	4B16; P-2	Inspect and replace power steering hoses and fittings.	C183	C183	19, 24
4B17; P-2	4B17; P-2	Inspect and replace pitman arm, relay (centerlink/intermediate) rod, idler arm and mountings, and steering linkage damper.	C184	C184	27-29
4B18; P-1	4B18; P-1	Inspect, replace, and adjust tie rod ends (sockets), tie rod sleeves, and clamps.	C185	C185	27, 29
4B19; P-3	4B19; P-3	Test and diagnose components of electronically controlled steering systems using a scan tool; determine necessary action.	C186	C186	67-69
4B20; P-3	4B20; P-3	Inspect and test electric power assist steering.	C700	C550	67-68
4B21; P-3	4B21; P-3	Identify hybrid vehicle power steering system electrical circuits, service and safety precautions.	C551	C551	67, 72

C. Suspension Systems Diagnosis and Repair					
NATEF 2008 Reference and Priority	NATEF 2005 Reference and Priority	Tasksheet Title	2008 CDX Tasksheet Number	2005 CDX Tasksheet Number	Page(s)
4C1; P-1	4C101; P-1	Diagnose short and long arm suspension system noises, body sway, and uneven ride height concerns; determine necessary action.	C852	C187	59-60
4C2; P-1	4C102; P-1	Diagnose strut suspension system noises, body sway, and uneven ride height concerns; determine necessary action.	C853	C188	59, 61

			2008 CDX	2005 CDX	
4C3; P-2	4C103; P-3	Remove, inspect, and install upper and lower control arms, bushings, shafts, and rebound bumpers.	C790	C189	45, 47–48, 51
4C4; P-2	4C104; P-2	Remove, inspect, and install strut rods and bushings.	C791	C190	53, 55–56
4C5; P-1	4C105; P-1	Remove, inspect, and install upper and/or lower ball joints.	C792	C191	45, 48–49
4C6; P-2	4C106; P-2	Remove, inspect, and install steering knuckle assemblies.	C192	C192	45, 47, 50
4C7; P-3	4C107; P-3	Remove, inspect, and install short and long arm suspension system coil springs and spring insulators.	C193	C193	45–47, 50
4C8; P-3	4C108; P-3	Remove, inspect, install, and adjust suspension system torsion bars; inspect mounts.	C194	C194	53, 56–57
4C9; P-2	4C109; P-2	Remove, inspect, and install stabilizer bar bushings, brackets, and links.	C793	C195	45–46, 50
4C10; P-1	4C110, 4C204; P-1, P-2	Remove, inspect, and install strut cartridge or assembly, strut coil spring, insulators (silencers), and upper strut bearing mount.	C794	C201, C196	53–55
N/A	4C201, 4C202; P-2	(Removed for 2008)	N/A	C198, C199	
4C11; P-3	4C203; P-3	Remove, inspect, and install leaf springs, leaf spring insulators (silencers), shackles, brackets, bushings, and mounts.	C854	C200	63–65

D. Related Suspension and Steering Service

NATEF 2008 Reference and Priority	NATEF 2005 Reference and Priority	Tasksheet Title	2008 CDX Tasksheet Number	2005 CDX Tasksheet Number	Page(s)
4D1; P-1	4C301; P-1	Inspect, remove, and replace shock absorbers.	C202	C202	63–64
4D2; P-1	4C302; P-1	Remove, inspect, and service or replace front and rear wheel bearings.	C203	C203	63, 65–66
4D3; P-3	4C303; P-3	Test and diagnose components of electronically controlled suspension systems using a scan tool; determine necessary action.	C204	C204	67, 72–73
4D4; P-3	N/A	Diagnose, inspect, adjust, repair or replace components of electronically controlled steering systems (including sensors, switches, and actuators); initialize system as required.	C614	N/A	67, 70–71
4D5; P-3	N/A	Describe the function of the idle speed compensation switch.	C615	N/A	67, 71
4D6; P-2	4C111; P-2	Lubricate suspension and steering systems.	C616	C197	45, 49–50

E. Wheel Alignment Diagnosis, Adjustment, and Repair

NATEF 2008 Reference and Priority	NATEF 2005 Reference and Priority	Tasksheet Title	2008 CDX Tasksheet Number	2005 CDX Tasksheet Number	Page(s)
4E1; P-1	4D01; P-1	Diagnose vehicle wander, drift, pull, hard steering, bump steer, memory steer, torque steer, and steering return concerns; determine necessary action.	C206	C206	75–76, 81–82
4E2; P-1	4D02, 4D03; P-1	Perform prealignment inspection and measure vehicle ride height; perform necessary action.	C617	C207, C208	75–77
4E3; P-1	4D04, 4D05, 4D06; P-1	Prepare vehicle for wheel alignment on the alignment machine; perform four wheel alignment by checking and adjusting front and rear wheel caster, camber, and toe as required; center steering wheel.	C618	C209, C210, C211	75, 77–78, 80
4E4; P-2	4D07; P-2	Check toe-out-on-turns (turning radius); determine necessary action.	C213	C213	75, 78, 81
4E5; P-2	4D08; P-2	Check SAI (steering axis inclination) and included angle; determine necessary action.	C214	C214	75, 78, 81
N/A	4D09; P-1	(Removed for 2008)	N/A	C215	
4E6; P-1	4D10; P-1	Check rear wheel thrust angle; determine necessary action.	C216	C216	75, 78–79, 81
4E7; P-2	4D11; P-2	Check for front wheel setback; determine necessary action.	C217	C217	75, 79–80
4E8; P-3	4D12; P-3	Check front and/or rear cradle (subframe) alignment; determine necessary action.	C795	C218	75, 82

F. Wheel and Tire Diagnosis and Repair

NATEF 2008 Reference and Priority	NATEF 2005 Reference and Priority	Tasksheet Title	2008 CDX Tasksheet Number	2005 CDX Tasksheet Number	Page(s)
4F1; P-1	4E01, 4E02; P-1	Inspect tire condition; identify tire wear patterns; check and adjust air pressure; determine necessary action.	C619	C219, C220	5-7
4F2; P-2	4E03; P-2	Diagnose wheel/tire vibration, shimmy, and noise; determine necessary action.	C855	C221	11, 15-16
4F3; P-1	4E04; P-1	Rotate tires according to manufacturer's recommendations.	C222	C222	5, 7-8
4F4; P-2	4E05; P-2	Measure wheel, tire, axle flange, and hub runout; determine necessary action.	C701	C223	11, 14-15
4F5; P-2	4E06; P-2	Diagnose tire pull problems; determine necessary action.	C796	C224	11, 16-17
N/A	4E07; P-1	(Removed for 2008)	N/A	C225	
4F6; P-1	4E08; P-2	Dismount, inspect, and remount tire on wheel; balance wheel and tire assembly (static and dynamic).	C620	C226	5, 8-9
4F7; P-2	4E09; P-3	Dismount, inspect, and remount tire on wheel equipped with tire pressure monitoring system sensor.	C621	C579	5, 9-10
4F8; P-1	4E10; P-1	Reinstall wheel; torque lug nuts.	C227	C227	5, 8
4F9; P-1	4E11; P-1	Inspect tire and wheel assembly for air loss; perform necessary action.	C580	C580	11-13
4F10; P-1	4E12; P-1	Repair tire using internal patch.	C552	C552	11, 13
4F11; P-2	4E13; P-3	Inspect, diagnose, and calibrate tire pressure monitoring system.	C553	C553	11, 13-14

Appendix B: Additional Suspension and Steering Tasksheets from 2005 NATEF Tasks

Student/intern information:

Name_____ Date_____ Class_____

Vehicle used for this activity:

Year_____ Make_____ Model_____

Odometer_____ VIN _____

© Jones and Bartlett Publishers, LLC

Learning Objective/Task	CDX Tasksheet Number	2005 NATEF Reference Number	2005 NATEF Priority Level
• Remove, inspect, and install coil springs and spring insulators.	C198	4C201	P-2
• Remove, inspect, and install transverse links, control arms, bushings, and mounts.	C199	4C202	P-2

Time off_____

Time on_____

Total time_____

Recommended Resource Materials

- CDX Automotive program
- CDX eTextbook
- Technical service bulletins, shop manuals, and any other information applicable to the specific vehicle or components you are working on
- Class notes

Materials Required

- Floor jack and safety stands
- Specialist steering and suspension toolkits
- Vehicle fitted with rear suspension unit with coil spring
- Vehicle fitted with rear suspension unit with transverse links, control arms, and suspension

Some Safety Issues to Consider

- Vehicle jacks and stands are important tools that increase productivity and make the job easier. But they can also cause severe injury or death if used improperly. Make sure you follow the jack and stand manufacturer's operation procedures. Also, make sure you have your supervisor/instructor's permission to use a vehicle jack or stand.
- Always wear the correct protective eyewear and clothing and use the appropriate safety equipment, as well as fender covers, seat protectors, and floor mat protectors.
- Make sure you understand and observe all legislative and personal safety procedures when carrying out practical assignments. If you are unsure of what these are, ask your supervisor/instructor.

Performance Standard

0—No exposure: No information or practice provided during the program; complete training required

1—Exposure only: General information provided with no practice time; close supervision needed; additional training required

2—Limited practice: Has practiced job during training program; additional training required to develop skill

3—Moderately skilled: Has performed job independently during training program; limited additional training may be required

4—Skilled: Can perform job independently with no additional training

▶ **TASK** Remove, inspect, and install coil springs and spring insulators. `C198 4C201`

1. Jack up the rear end of the vehicle in the correct jacking position as indicated in the shop manual. Place the safety stands in position as indicated in the manual to carry out rear suspension component removal.

2. Have your supervisor/instructor verify this action.
   a. Supervisor/instructor initials: _____

3. Lower the vehicle onto the jack stands. After lowering the vehicle onto the safety stands and with the jack still supporting minimal vehicle weight, check the safety stands to ensure they are supporting the vehicle weight correctly.

Time off_____

Time on_____

Total time_____

4. Have your supervisor/instructor verify this action.
   a. Supervisor/instructor initials: _____

5. Completely lower the jack.

6. Following the instructions and all the safety precautions outlined in the shop manual, remove the coil spring and insulators. Place components on the work bench for evaluation.

7. With reference to the appropriate shop manual section, inspect and record the condition of the following components.
   a. Coil seat insulators: _____
   b. Coil spring: _____

8. Following the instructions and all the safety precautions outlined in the shop manual, install insulators. Re-assemble coil spring suspension components. Torque all retaining bolts to the manufacturer's specifications (if applicable).
   a. Record the torque settings used: _____

9. Jack the vehicle and remove the safety stands. Lower the vehicle to the ground.

10. Return the vehicle to its beginning condition and clean and return any tools that you may have used to their proper locations.

11. Have your supervisor/instructor verify satisfactory completion of this procedure, any observations found, and any necessary action/s recommended.

Performance Rating

CDX Tasksheet Number: C198   2005 NATEF Reference Number: 4C201

☐	☐	☐	☐	☐
0	1	2	3	4

Supervisor/instructor signature _____ Date _____

▶ **TASK** Remove, inspect, and install transverse links, control arms, bushings, and mounts.

C199 4C202

Vehicle used for this activity:

Year_____ Make_____ Model_____

Odometer_____ VIN _____

1. Jack up the rear end of the vehicle in the correct jacking position as indicated in the shop manual. Place the safety stands in position as indicated in the manual to carry out rear suspension component removal.

2. Have your supervisor/instructor verify this action.
   a. Supervisor/instructor initials: _____

3. Lower the vehicle onto the jack stands. After lowering the vehicle onto the safety stands and with the jack still supporting minimal vehicle weight, check the safety stands to ensure they are supporting the vehicle weight correctly.

4. Have your supervisor/instructor verify this action.
   a. Supervisor/instructor initials: _____

5. Completely lower the jack.

6. Following the instructions and all the safety precautions outlined in the shop manual, remove the transverse link/s, control arm/s, and bushings. Place components on the work bench for evaluation.

7. With reference to the appropriate shop manual section, inspect and record the condition of the following components.
   a. Bushings: _____
   b. Control arms: _____
   c. Mounting/s brackets: _____
   d. Transverse links: _____

8. Following the instructions and all the safety precautions outlined in the shop manual, install insulators. Re-assemble coil spring suspension components. Torque all retaining bolts to the manufacturer's specifications (if applicable).
   a. Record the torque settings used: _____

9. Jack the vehicle and remove the safety stands. Lower the vehicle to the ground.

10. Return the vehicle to its beginning condition and clean and return any tools that you may have used to their proper locations.

11. Have your supervisor/instructor verify satisfactory completion of this procedure, any observations found, and any necessary action/s recommended.

Performance Rating

CDX Tasksheet Number: C199   2005 NATEF Reference Number: 4C202

☐	☐	☐	☐	☐
0	1	2	3	4

Supervisor/instructor signature _____ Date_____

Student/intern information:

Name_____ Date_____ Class_____

Vehicle used for this activity:

Year_____ Make_____ Model_____

Odometer_____ VIN _____

Learning Objective/Task	CDX Tasksheet Number	2005 NATEF Reference Number	2005 NATEF Priority Level
• Check and adjust rear wheel toe.	C215	4D09	P-1

Recommended Resource Materials

- CDX Automotive program
- CDX eTextbook
- Technical service bulletins, shop manuals, and any other information applicable to the specific vehicle or components you are working on
- Class notes

Materials Required

- Appropriate wheel alignment equipment and operator's manual
- Floor jack and safety stands
- Specialist steering and suspension toolkits

Some Safety Issues to Consider

- Lifting equipment such as vehicle jacks and stands, vehicle hoists, and engine hoists are important tools that increase productivity and make the job easier. But they can also cause severe injury or death if used improperly. Make sure you follow the manufacturer's operation procedures. Also, make sure you have your supervisor/ instructor's permission to use any particular type of lifting equipment.
- Always wear the correct protective eyewear and clothing and use the appropriate safety equipment, as well as fender covers, seat protectors, and floor mat protectors.
- Make sure that you understand and observe all legislative and personal safety procedures when carrying out practical assignments. If you are unsure of what these are, check with your supervisor/instructor.

Performance Standard

0–No exposure: No information or practice provided during the program; complete training required

1–Exposure only: General information provided with no practice time; close supervision needed; additional training required

2–Limited practice: Has practiced job during training program; additional training required to develop skill

3–Moderately skilled: Has performed job independently during training program; limited additional training may be required

4–Skilled: Can perform job independently with no additional training

▶ **TASK** Check and adjust rear wheel toe.   C215 4D09

1. Check, adjust, and record the tire pressure readings for the make and model of the vehicle you will be working on.
   a. Brand of tire:
      i.   Left front: _____
      ii. Right front: _____
      iii. Right rear: _____
      iv. Left rear: _____
   b. Tire size: _____
      i.   Are all sizes as per the manufacturer's recommendations? **Yes/No** (Circle one)
   c. Maker's specifications:
      i.   Recommended pressure: _____
      ii. Inflated tire pressure: _____

2. Carry out an inspection of the vehicle's tires for any abnormal wear patterns as described in the appropriate section of the shop manual.
   i. Left front tire: _____
   ii. Right front tire: _____
   iii. Right rear tire: _____
   iv. Left rear tire: _____
3. As outlined in the appropriate section of the shop manual, record the manufacturer's recommended ride height. List the specifications:

4. As outlined in the appropriate section of the shop manual, carry out and record the ride height of this vehicle. List your findings:

5. As outlined in the instruction manual for the type of alignment equipment being used, place the vehicle in the correct position to enable the front end suspension alignment specifications to be evaluated.

NOTE ▶ Ensure you are following all the safety precautions listed by the equipment and vehicle manufacturer for this procedure.

6. Have your supervisor/instructor verify this action.
   a. Supervisor/instructor initials: _____
7. Check and adjust if necessary the rear wheel toe, as described in the appropriate section of the shop manual.
   a. Manufacturer's specification for rear wheel toe: _____
   b. Record your findings and final settings:

   c. Have your supervisor/instructor verify these findings.
      i. Supervisor/instructor initials: _____
8. Remove the vehicle from the alignment equipment.
9. Discuss these findings/concerns with your supervisor/instructor and what action needs to be taken to rectify the situation.
10. Return the vehicle to its beginning condition and clean and return any tools that you may have used to their proper locations.
11. Have your supervisor/instructor verify satisfactory completion of this procedure, any observations found, and any necessary action/s recommended.

Performance Rating

		CDX Tasksheet Number: C215	**2005 NATEF Reference Number: 4D09**	
☐	☐	☐	☐	☐
0	1	2	3	4

Supervisor/instructor signature _____ Date_____

Student/intern information:

Name_____ Date_____ Class_____

Vehicle used for this activity:

Year_____ Make_____ Model_____

Odometer_____ VIN _____

Learning Objective/Task	CDX Tasksheet Number	2005 NATEF Reference Number	2005 NATEF Priority Level
• Balance wheel and tire assembly (static and dynamic).	C225	4E07	P-1

Recommended Resource Materials

- CDX Automotive program
- CDX eTextbook
- Technical service bulletins, shop manuals, and any other information applicable to the specific vehicle or components you are working on
- Class notes

Materials Required

- Vehicle (or wheel/tire assembly)
- Vehicle hoist or floor jack and jack stand
- Tire pressure gauge
- Tire inflator
- Wheel balancer
- Wheel weight hammer
- Wheel weight selection

Some Safety Issues to Consider

- Vehicle hoists are important tools that increase productivity and make the job easier. But they also can cause severe injury or death if used improperly. Make sure you follow the hoist and vehicle manufacturer's operation procedures. Also, make sure you have your supervisor/instructor's permission to use a vehicle hoist.
- Worn or damaged tires may have steel cords sticking out of the tire. These wires are very sharp and will severely cut you. Do not rub your hand across a tire without first checking for exposed cords.
- Compressed air can be very dangerous. Never blow it at someone. Never use it to remove dirt or dust from your skin or clothing. Never use it without an OSHA-approved nozzle.
- You may be working under the hood of a running vehicle. Keep your hands and fingers away from moving belts, fans, and other parts.
- Over-inflating tires could cause the tire to explode with great force. Never exceed the maximum tire pressure for the tire you are working on.
- Always wear the correct protective eyewear and clothing and use the appropriate safety equipment, as well as fender covers, seat protectors, and floor mat protectors.
- Make sure that you understand and observe all legislative and personal safety procedures when carrying out practical assignments. If you are unsure of what these are, check with your supervisor/instructor.

Performance Standard

0—No exposure: No information or practice provided during the program; complete training required

1—Exposure only: General information provided with no practice time; close supervision needed; additional training required

2—Limited practice: Has practiced job during training program; additional training required to develop skill

3—Moderately skilled: Has performed job independently during training program; limited additional training may be required

4—Skilled: Can perform job independently with no additional training

© Jones and Bartlett Publishers, LLC

▶ TASK Balance wheel and tire assembly (static and dynamic). **C225 4E07**

Time off_____

Time on_____

Total time_____

1. Research the proper lug nut torque and torque pattern for this vehicle in an appropriate manual.
   a. Lug nut torque: _____ ft-lbs/Nm
   b. Draw the lug nut torque pattern for this vehicle.

2. If necessary, remove the wheel from the vehicle.

> **NOTE ▶** When removing hub caps and wheels, please store them in such a manner as not to damage the visible side of the hub cap or wheel. Laying them face down will cause them to become scratched and damaged. Also, store the lug nuts so they will not get lost or kicked.

3. Remove all wheel weights from the rim.

4. Check tire pressure. Make sure it is at the proper pressure before attempting to balance it.

5. Mount the wheel/tire on a balancer according to the manufacturer's procedure.

6. Calibrate the balancer to the wheel/tire assembly.

7. Check the balance of the wheel/tire and list the amount it is out of balance:
   a. Inside of the rim: _____ oz/grams
   b. Outside of the rim: _____ oz/grams

8. Add the appropriate wheel weights to the appropriate spots on the rim.

9. Recheck the balance. If it is more than 0.2 oz (6 grams) out of balance, remove the weights and try to re-balance it. If it is not more than 0.2 oz (6 grams) out of balance on each side, call your supervisor/instructor over to verify the reading.
   a. Supervisor/instructor's initials: _____

10. Reinstall the wheel/tire assembly, if appropriate.

11. Torque the lug nuts to the proper torque.

12. Reinstall the hub caps, if equipped. Insure that they are fully seated to prevent them from falling off while driving. If in doubt, ask your supervisor/instructor.

13. Return the vehicle to its beginning condition and return any tools that you may have used to their proper locations.

14. Have your supervisor/instructor verify satisfactory completion of this procedure, any observations found, and any necessary action/s recommended.

Performance Rating

CDX Tasksheet Number: C225   2005 NATEF Reference Number: 4E07

☐	☐	☐	☐	☐
0	1	2	3	4

Supervisor/instructor signature _____ Date_____